The Complete Jewish Wedding Planner

presented on the occasion of

The Wedding of

_____

and

_____

on

_____

at

_____

The

Complete

Jewish

Wedding

Planner

WENDY CHERNAK HEFTER

PSP Press, Inc.
Baltimore, Maryland

My warmest thanks are extended to some special
family and friends who helped create this book:

David Hefter, my husband and best friend, who devoted
    countless hours to editing and producing this book
    on our home computer system
Judy Esterson Chernak, my mom, for her original
    exhaustive editing and her continuous moral support
Debi Chernak, my sister, for her thorough proofreading
Rabbi Mitchell Wohlberg of Beth Tfiloh Congregation
    (Baltimore, Maryland) and Rabbi Bernard Rothman
    of Congregation Sons of Israel (Cherry Hill, New
    Jersey) for reviewing the Jewish aspects discussed
    and for making valuable contributions
Dr. Sidney I. Esterson, my grandfather of blessed
    memory, for technical editing of the Hebrew material

THE COMPLETE JEWISH WEDDING PLANNER.

Copyright © 1986, 1988, 1992, 1993, 1997

For information contact: PSP Press, Inc., 101 Brightside Avenue
                            Baltimore, MD 21208-4804

THIRD EDITION

Designer: Thomas Ingalls & Associates

Library of Congress Catalog Card Number: 92-81988

Hefter, Wendy Chernak.

    The complete Jewish wedding planner.

    Bibliography: p.193
    1. Marriage customs and rites, Jewish.
    2. Wedding etiquette. I. Title.

ISBN 0-96-357530-9 (previously ISBN 0-06-250377-4)

To David, with whom I shared this wonderful personal experience and who supported this book from day one; to my mom and dad, Judy and Ted, for their enthusiasm and help in planning every detail of our wedding, a *simcha* full of *mazel* and *nachas*; and to my in-laws, Ruth and Sy, who are responsible for bringing David into the world.

CONTENTS

Introduction

This workbook was created to help the Jewish bride and groom and their families with the planning of their wedding--from engagement through *Sheva Berachot*, the week following the ceremony. An array of Jewish and American customs is included to give you the option of learning about traditions you may otherwise not come across. The Grand Checklist calms your planning worries by keeping you on a realistic schedule. Next, lists and charts are designed to encourage you to ask appropriate questions when evaluating each service essential to your *simcha* ("joyous occasion"). Several pages are duplicated to aid you in comparison shopping. Not every list or chart will be valid or totally applicable to each couple--you need only to skip these pages. There are blank guest lists, a "wish list" of gift selections, and even complete checklists for the wedding day itself.

Using this book, any bride, groom, or relative of the couple can plan any wedding--from a secular to a very Orthodox Jewish wedding--without having to look elsewhere for more information. A few details not included may be obtained from readily available sources and have been so indicated. And the Glossary in the back can assist you with unfamiliar terms.

My husband, David, joins me in wishing you much *nachas* ("joy") on this most significant *simcha*. Remember: Perfection is unattainable and impossible! Cherish everything about your special day with the knowledge that the minor deviations from your "perfect plans" will be the spices that flavor your wedding and make it truly unique.

WENDY CHERNAK HEFTER
January 1997

NOTES

Part I

Wedding Traditions— Jewish and American

Your wedding is one of the most exciting days in your life, and it should be as close to your (and your parents') dreams as possible. Choosing among the traditions will give you an opportunity to reflect the respective beliefs and backgrounds of the bride and groom and your families. As you read this section, consider your emotions on the days following your wedding day: will you relive the day, view the video, and be proud of your wedding and the customs you chose to include? Will you have considered the wishes of your dear ones and also fashioned a *simcha* that fits you? Let's hope your answers are yes!

SIGNIFICANCE OF MARRIAGE

Wedding Day

As your wedding day approaches, you feel very excited...and you should! According to Jewish law, marriage is not only a privilege: it is also a responsibility. God said to Adam, "It is not good that the man should be alone; I will make him a companion" (Genesis 2:18). He then created Eve from Adam's rib and gave her to him as a partner. God wanted this union to be natural and wanted Adam always to feel that his wife, Eve, was a part of him. The **Talmud** also stresses the importance of marriage: "One who does not have a wife lives without joy, without bliss, without happiness" (Yevamot 62b). The **Shulchan Aruch** (Code of Jewish Law) states that it is our duty to get married in order to "Be fruitful and multiply," "*Pe'ru urevu*" (Genesis 1:28). The strong, loving family unit is of paramount importance in Jewish tradition.

The Matchmaker

Tradition says that forty days before your birth God decides whom you will marry. In ancient times, there was a matchmaker, a **shadchan**, to arrange marriages. The *shadchan* would travel between cities and propose the matches because the Jews had limited mobility and would otherwise have been restricted to marrying within their own community. Although travel is easy today for most people, the *shadchan* still exists in the form of matchmaking services and marriage bureaus, which are thriving nationwide. But you are past that stage by now!

Because each person deserves individual attention and celebration at this time in her or his life, there is a prohibition against having two siblings marry on the same day. Each *simcha* deserves its own recognition and rejoicing, so as not to lessen the importance of one for the other. In Genesis 29:27, Jacob was instructed to celebrate the entire week after he was tricked into marrying Leah--"Fulfill the week of this one"--before he could also marry her sister Rachel, whom he loved. (Their father would not disgrace Leah by marrying off his younger daughter first, in keeping with the tradition of the times.) Here again the importance of *each* marriage is stressed, as is the deep respect Jews have for their *simchas*.*
(*Note*: A double wedding of siblings may be scheduled in the evening so that one is married before sundown and one after--two different Hebrew dates--as my mother and her sister did. Halachically [according to Jewish law], the *reception* for the first sibling should also be completed before the second ceremony proceeds; in actual practice, usually only the *ceremonies* are separated by sundown.)

---

*Yiddish plural of *simcha*, more commonly used than Hebrew plural *semachot*.

THE WEDDING DAY

In preparation for this most important day, the bride and groom traditionally fast and repent as they do on **Yom Kippur**, the Day of Atonement. If the ceremony is in the evening, the bride and groom may eat a light snack beforehand when the stars come out, as that is the beginning of the next Hebrew day. Fasting is prohibited on these festive days: **Rosh Chodesh** (first day of a new Hebrew month), the day after **Shavuot** (Pentecost), the fifteenth day of the month of **Av**, the fifteenth of **Shevat**, **Chanukah**, **Purim**, **Shushan Purim**, and the fourteenth and fifteenth days of **Adar I** in a leap year. (*Note:* Purim occurs on the fourteenth of Adar, Shushan Purim on the fifteenth. Seven times each nineteen years, a second month of Adar is added to the calendar. Even though Purim is celebrated in Adar II during leap years, the fourteenth and fifteenth days of Adar I are still considered to have a festive aspect; therefore, fasting is prohibited.)

The bride and groom are then ready to enter this new stage of life together after serious reflection and purification. The idea of purity is the basis for the bride's white gown, as well as for the **kittel**, the white robe the groom may wear during the wedding ceremony. It reflects the solemnity of the wedding day, as well as other solemn occasions throughout his lifetime, such as Yom Kippur and the **Pesach Seder**. (Both men and women are also buried in white garments.)

BEFORE THE CEREMONY

Because the bride and groom are not supposed to see each other until the ceremonial veiling of the bride, separate receptions are held for them as the guests are arriving at the ceremony site. The **Kabbalat Panim** (literally, "Greeting Faces") is the groom's reception for male guests, although females are welcomed, too. (In Yiddish this is called **Chossen's Tish**, "Groom's Table.") The guests listen to a **d'var Torah**, a short Torah lesson, by the groom or a designated relative or friend.

In some circles, it is customary to read and sign the **tena'im** (literally, "conditions") at the groom's reception. This formal contract announces the wedding date and sets forth various prenuptial agreements, including a fee to be paid by the groom to the bride's father. In ancient times, the Tena'im were often arranged when children were very young, to ensure the continuity of the family. However, because it is a witnessed agreement and a broken engagement may cause legal problems, today the Tena'im ceremony is performed immediately before the wedding ceremony. The rabbi will provide the paper if you choose to include this ceremony.

At the conclusion of the Tena'im ceremony, the mothers, having joined the guests at the groom's reception, wrap a piece of fine pottery or china in a cloth and break it on the corner of a chair. The mothers retain a piece for themselves as good luck and distribute the broken pieces to unmarried women as a wish that they may also have a joyous wedding. A similar American custom is throwing the bouquet and garter.

Next, the **ketubbah**, having previously been reviewed by the rabbi, is displayed. The *ketubbah* is the Jewish legal contract that states the obligations of the groom to his bride in marriage, death, and divorce. The original Aramaic text was developed in the second century B.C.E., although the oldest *ketubbah* found dates back to the fifth century B.C.E. Standards were created by the **Sephardim** in the eleventh century and by the **Ashkenazim** in the twelfth century. Although printed *ketubbot* (plural) are available with Orthodox, Conservative, Reform, and Egalitarian texts, many couples decide to invest in a genuine piece of artwork and commission an experienced scribe, a **sofer**. This Hebrew artist-calligrapher will design an individual *ketubbah* after an interview with the couple and will hand-letter the text in Aramaic on request.

Then the groom designates two witnesses, **edim** (singular: **ed**), who must be Jewish males over **Bar Mitzvah** age (thirteen) and **Shomer Shabbat**, "Sabbath observant," and unrelated to the bride, the groom, and to each other. Next, the groom accepts a handkerchief from the rabbi to symbolize his formal acceptance of the responsibilities set forth in the *ketubbah*; this ceremony is called the **Kinyan**. At this point, the last word of the *ketubbah* (*ve'kanina*, "I have made a *kinyan*") is written, and formal acceptance of the *ketubbah* and its contents is completed. (*Note:* If the *sofer* who created your *ketubbah* is not present at the *Kabbalat Panim*, he or she will have left only the last stroke of the Hebrew letter *Kuf* in the word *ve'kanina* to be completed, or one letter outlined to be filled in.)

The two witnesses sign the *ketubbah* in which the groom, the **chatan** (or **chossen** in Yiddish), promises to provide food, shelter, and conjugal relations to his bride, the **kallah**. The groom presents the *ketubbah* to the bride at the ceremony. According to *Halacha*, the couple can live together only if the bride has the *ketubbah* in her possession and knows its whereabouts at all times. Many couples put a photograph of the *ketubbah* in their safe deposit box and display the original in their home.

During the Kabbalat Panim, the women have been pampering and entertaining the bride, **Hachnasat Kallah**. Attending the bride is an honor and called a *mitzvah*, "good deed." This is the time for the women to compliment the bride on her beauty and her special glow--"*Kallah na'eh va'chasudah*"--and to wish her well as she sits in her **kisei kallah**, "bridal throne," awaiting her groom and the **Badeken die Kallah**, "Veiling of the Bride." The Badeken has its origin in the story of Rebecca in the Book of Genesis. Isaac sent his servant Eliezer to find him a bride, and he chose Rebecca. As they journeyed home, they saw Isaac coming to meet them. Rebecca asked, "What man is this that walks in the field to meet us?" And the servant replied, "It is my master [Isaac]" (Genesis 24:64-65), whereupon Rebecca took her veil and covered her face in the ancient Eastern tradition of modesty. The Badeken ceremony occurs only for a bride's first marriage.

The groom is escorted by the male guests from the Kabbalat Panim to the bride for the Badeken. As he covers her face with the veil, the rabbi says, "Our sister! Be thou the mother of thousands of ten thousands" (Genesis 24:60). The parents then bless the bride and groom, and the guests are requested to seat themselves in preparation for the ceremony. (*Note*: The American tradition has the ushers seat the guests.)

THE PROCESSIONAL AND THE *CHUPPAH*

The bride and groom are like queen and king on their wedding day, so they are escorted down the aisle by an entourage of attendants, **shoshvinim**. (Ancient northern European history tells a different tale of the attendants. The custom was for the groom to raid the village in which the bride lived and carry her away. The best man and the groomsmen held back the relatives, and the bridesmaids tried to protect the bride from capture. If the raid was successful, the groomsmen received gifts for their services. The bridesmaids had already been bribed to allow the groom to capture his bride!)

The Jewish processional is slightly different from the traditional American processional, although it is common practice for each member of any processional to start down the aisle on the *right* foot! The rabbi and cantor enter first, followed by the bride's grandparents, then the groom's grandparents. The ushers, best man, and ring bearer(s) follow, in that order, to introduce the groom and his parents. (The mothers are on the right side when walking down the aisle.) In very Orthodox or Sephardic weddings, the groom is escorted by the two fathers--and the bride by the two mothers--in keeping with **tzniut**, "modesty," and the laws of separation of males and females in public. Otherwise, as in the Ashkenazic custom, both parents escort their child down the aisle to share in the pride and honor of "giving their child away." The bridesmaids, maid or matron of honor, and flower girl(s) enter before the bride and her parents.

Candles

The procession toward the wedding canopy may be illuminated by candles. There are several explanations for this tradition. The light emitted from the candles represents the lightning that appeared when Israel (the bride) accepted God (the groom), light being a symbol of God's presence. Another interpretation explains the similarity of the wedding lights to those of the candles kindled on the **Shabbat** and on the **yomim tovim**, "holidays." The Book of Esther (8:16) says, "The Jews had light and gladness and joy and honor," *"Orah ve'simchah ve'sasson ve'yikar."* Last, the sum of the letters of the Hebrew word for candle, *ner*, multiplied by 2, the number of witnesses required for the wedding (or the bride and the groom equals 2), results in the numerical value of the sum of the letters of the beautiful phrase, *"Pe'ru ure'vu,"* "Be fruitful and multiply."

The Wedding Canopy

The groom walks to the **chuppah**, the wedding canopy, first so he can receive his bride, as God received Israel. Another reason he arrives first is that the *chuppah* represents the room in the groom's home where the marriage will be consummated; thus, he is bringing his bride into the wedding chamber. Sometimes the couple will choose to hold the Chuppah (used here synonymously with "wedding ceremony") outside, a practice based on the verse, "Thus [like the stars] shall your children be" (Exodus 15:5).

The *chuppah* is usually made from fine cloth, such as velvet or silk, and is beautifully decorated with embroidery and/or flowers. A **tallit**, or prayer shawl, can also be used as the *chuppah*. This tradition originated in the seventeenth century in Germany and France where the *tallit* was spread around the bride and groom.

The handmade *chuppah* or *tallit* is spread over four poles--one at each corner--but does not extend over the edges. These poles may be held by honored friends or family. Most synagogues own a *chuppah* whose poles are temporarily secured on the floor for the ceremony.

Who Stands Under

the Canopy

Usually all members of the procession stand under the *chuppah*, although grandparents and young children often prefer to sit in the first row. Those who are under the *chuppah* arrange themselves thus:

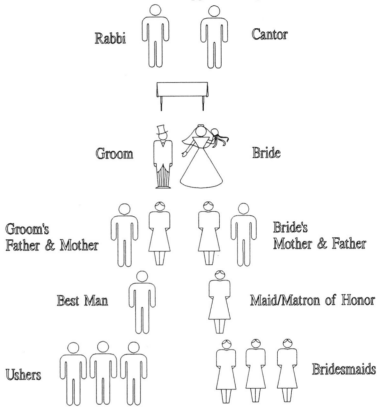

The *Chasidic* bride and groom usually face their guests; therefore, this arrangement would be reversed: the groom, with the bride on his right, exchanging places with the rabbi and cantor. (Guests may sit on the same side as the bride or groom, depending on whose guest they are.)

THE CEREMONY

Before the bride takes her position next to the groom, she may circle him either three or seven times: "The prophet says that a woman encompasses and protects a man" (Jeremiah 31:21). Again, the interpretations are numerous. The most accepted reason for the number 3 is that God (the groom) said to Israel (the bride), "And I will betroth you unto Me forever; and I will betroth you unto Me in righteousness, and in justice, and in lovingkindness, and in compassion; and I will betroth you unto Me in faithfulness, and you shall know the Lord" (Hosea 2:21-22). The words *"and I will betroth you," "ve'erastich,"* are used here three times. Also, three obligations of the man to his wife are stated in the *ketubbah*: food, clothing, and conjugal rights. The **tefillin**, "phylactery," straps are wrapped around the middle finger three times every morning during prayer. There are three **aliyot**, "Torah honors," during the weekday Torah readings. And there are three Halachic requirements of marriage (discussed in the next section).

The Bride Circles the Groom

The number 7 also occurs frequently in Jewish history: seven days in the week; the seventh day is the Sabbath, seven *aliyot* are given out on the Sabbath; seven **hakafot**, "processionals," on **Hoshanah Rabbah**, seventh day of **Sukkot**; seven repetitions in the Bible of the phrase "and when a man takes a wife"; and seven blessings, the **Sheva Berachot**, during the wedding ceremony.

When the bride, followed by the mothers, has completed her circles, she takes her place to the right of the groom: "At thy right hand doth stand the Queen. . ." (Psalms 45:10). This is also the rationale for the mothers' walking down the aisle on the right.

Next, the cantor sings a short hymn, which serves as the start of the **Erusin**, "Engagement," ceremony. The rabbi recites the blessing over the wine and then the betrothal blessing, **Birkat Erusin**. The groom drinks some of the wine and then hands the cup to the bride, whose veil has been lifted by her mother or the maid/matron of honor. Drinking from the same glass indicates that the bride and groom are ready to begin a life of sharing.

Engagement Ceremony

Betrothal Blessing

The engagement ceremony is also often referred to as **Kiddushin**. The *Kiddushin* proceeds with the first of the three Halachic requirements for a marriage which are: *tabba'at* (ring)/*kesef* (money), *shetar* (deed or bride's acceptance), and *yichud* (seclusion)/*bi'ah* (consummation). First, the groom must give the bride something of value, usually the ring. The ring, **tabba'at**, represents the gold or silver, **kesef**, which was given to the bride in ancient times (beginning around the seventh century). The ring must be plain metal, preferably gold, without any stones, because the value of the ring must be easily determinable. Otherwise, the bride may over- or underestimate its worth, which would invalidate her acceptance of it and would thereby make the marriage null and void. The ring must be whole, **shlemut**, similar to the result of a union of two people, and its value must equal at least one *perutah*, the smallest coin in ancient times.

The Ring

Before putting the ring on the bride's finger, the groom recites the **Harei At**, the public proclamation of this union:

Public Proclamation

> *Harei at me'kudeshet li b'tabba'at zu ke'dat Moshe ve'Yisrael.*
> Behold, you are consecrated unto me with this ring, in accordance with the law of Moses and Israel.

The Harei At is taken from the Talmud (Kiddushin 8a) and is very appropriate to this part of the wedding. There are thirty-two letters in the sentence. The Hebrew letters that make up the number 32 are *Lamed* (30) and *Bet/Vet* (2), and these two letters together spell *lev*, the Hebrew word for "heart." As he gives the bride the ring, the groom simultaneously gives her his heart. He places the ring on the forefinger of the bride's right hand (not over a gloved finger) so that it may be seen easily by the two appointed witnesses and by the guests. The ring may then be transferred to the ring finger of the left hand. This custom is based on the Greek belief that there is a vein in this finger that runs directly to the heart.

Bride's Acceptance

The second requirement is **shetar**, the deed, or bride's public acceptance of the ring (allowing the groom to put the ring on her finger) because, Halachically, the groom "takes a wife." If the bride chooses to give the groom a ring also, she may do so and recite the beautiful phrase:

> *Ani le'dodi ve'dodi li.*
> I am my beloved's and my beloved is mine.
>
> (Song of Songs 6:3)

This phrase is simply a statement of her affection and is not intended to be an "exchange." In fact, she could give him the ring during *Yichud* (discussed later). Some brides, during a Conservative or Reform ceremony, give the groom a ring and say, *"Harei ata me'kudash li"* (the masculine form of Harei At). This phrase implies that *she* is "taking" him as her husband; for this reason, it is not included in an Orthodox ceremony. In fact, some Orthodox rabbis will not perform a double-ring ceremony at all because it may be misconstrued.

The double-ring ceremony developed in America around World War II. Women began giving their husbands rings to announce to the women overseas that these men were "taken." This is a reverse of the medieval practice of departing knights locking their wives into chastity belts!

Reading of the Ketubbah

The Wedding Ceremony

The bride's acceptance of her ring marks the end of the betrothal ceremony, *Erusin*. At this natural break between Kiddushin and **Nissuin**, "the wedding ceremony," the *ketubbah* is read aloud in Aramaic (or Hebrew) and English and then given to the bride to keep. The rabbi usually makes some personal comments at this time, often incorporating a modern English translation of the **Sheva Berachot**, the seven marriage blessings.

The Seven Blessings

The *Nissuin* begins with the Sheva Berachot, also called the **Birkat Chatanim**, "Blessing for Grooms," which were extracted from the Talmud (Ketubbah 8a). Although only two witnesses are necessary for the Erusin, a *minyan*--ten men over Bar Mitzvah age--must be present for the Nissuin. The cantor usually recites all seven *berachot*, especially the last blessing, because beautiful melodies have been composed for it. A wonderful tradition is to honor fathers, grandfathers, uncles, and others by having them each recite one *beracha* (singular). Often, at Chasidic weddings, all seven *berachot* are recited by rabbis. Each *beracha* has its own significance: the first is for the wine; the second is in honor of the wedding guests; the third celebrates the creation of Adam; the fourth, fifth, and sixth bless the couple's marriage; and the seventh is in honor of Israel and the wedding couple.

The bride and groom share wine again--either from a second cup or from the refilled first cup. Two cups are used as a reminder of the two separate ceremonies (betrothal and marriage) occurring at this one time, but one cup is sufficient if it has been refilled before the Nissuin ceremony. *The Two Cups*

Many couples choose to include these few words added by the rabbi: "By the power vested in me by the state of (your state) and according to the traditions of Moses and Israel, I now pronounce you husband and wife." Before the groom kisses his bride, he breaks with his right foot a small glass that has been wrapped in a napkinor a special velvet pouch. This breakage suggests that a broken marriage cannot be easily repaired. It also serves as a reminder of the Destruction of the Temple: the bride and groom must always remember the sorrows of the Jewish people, even during *simchas*. The Talmud (Berachot 31a) tells us the story of a wedding celebration at which the guests included many rabbis. At one point during the *se'udah*, "festive meal," one rabbi smashed an expensive vase in order to warn the celebrants against limitless joy. (*Note*: A similar American custom is observed at bachelor parties: after the best man has toasted the bride and groom, he and all the men smash their glasses, so that they may never be used for a "less noble purpose.") At the sound of the broken glass, family and guests call out words of congratulations and *Mazel Tov* ("good luck"). (*Note*: Mazel, the Yiddish pronunciation of "luck," is more commonly used than the Hebrew pronunciation, maz*al*.) In Eastern Europe and Sephardic communities, at this point the couple try to step on each other's foot first to determine who will be the dominant one in the marriage! *Breaking the Glass*

AFTER THE CEREMONY

The third and final Halachic requirement for the bride and groom is **Yichud**, "seclusion," or **Bi'ah**, "consummation." First the couple leads the recessional, followed by (in this order) the bride's parents, the groom's parents, the maid or matron of honor and the best man, the ushers and the bridesmaids, the flower girl(s) and the ring bearer(s), and the rabbi and the cantor. (Here, too, the men and women walk separately, except for the bride and groom, if following strict Orthodox tradition.) This "entourage" escorts the queen and king (bride and groom) to a special room (the bride's room or the rabbi's study) so the couple can share a few private moments and break their fast together. Yichud/Bi'ah represents the time when, historically, the groom took his bride home to consummate the marriage. As this is an important ritual, two witnesses stand outside the door to keep well-wishers out for about ten minutes. *Recessional and Seclusion/Consummation*

Meanwhile, the guests are directed to the area where cocktails are being served. The family members and attendants mingle with the guests when they are not involved in the family photography session taking place concurrently in another room. If the bride and groom have not seen each other prior to the ceremony, this thirty- to forty-minute period during the cocktail hour offers the ideal time for the formal family photographs with the couple. Try to be as brief and efficient as possible--your guests are eager to congratulate you! *Photography Session*

THE RECEPTION

The Festive Meal

At the conclusion of the photo session, the bride and groom join the **se'udah** (festive meal, celebration). Upon their entrance into the reception hall, they are usually introduced as "the new Mr. and Mrs. (the groom's name)." (If the bride prefers a different form, such as "the new married couple, Ms. Miriam Goldstein and Mr. Eric Green," be sure to notify your bandleader!) Not until much later, when they see their photographs and video, do they really have a chance to appreciate the results of the months of planning and collaboration with their family members; for, before they have time to breathe, the bride and groom are whisked into the middle of the room for energetic and enthusiastic circle dancing. This is called the *Mitzvah L'Sameach Chatan V'Kallah* to make the groom and bride happy. (The men and women will dance in separate circles at Orthodox receptions.)

At one point, the bride and groom are lifted up into the air in individual chairs. Each grabs onto the side of his or her chair while attempting simultaneously to hold a corner of the same handkerchief! The handker-chief symbolizes their union but does not disobey the rules of *tzniut* (modesty) because their hands do not touch.

The dancers finally bring the chairs down to the floor and--when everyone is totally exhausted--the circles break up, and the bride and groom proceed to the front of the room for the **motzi**, blessing over the **challah**. (Observant Jews will wash their hands and recite the appropriate blessing before saying the *motzi*.) Finally, the couple sits down for a few moments to enjoy the meal. In between courses and dancing, the bride and groom should try to visit each table to greet the guests and pose for the table photographs.

Toasting the Couple

At a natural break in the excitement, some American customs may be included. First, the best man and/or the father(s) will toast the happy couple. There is no limit to the number of toasts, nor is there any restriction as to who may toast the couple. These toasts may signal the beginning of frequent calls for kisses: tapping spoons on the water glasses is a hint for the bride and groom to kiss. The more your guests tap, the more kisses you will get to share with your new spouse! Finally, the best man reads aloud any telegrams received for the bride and groom. (Having the reception videotaped is one way to remember the sentiments of these moments.)

The Dance of the Last Child

If either the bride or groom is the last child in the family to be wed, the **Mezinke Tanz**, one of the most exciting and touching traditions, is now danced to honor the occasion. The couple places a wreath of flowers on the mother's head and then dances around both parents, who are seated in chairs. The Yiddish song, *"Die Mezinke Oysgegeben,"* "The Youngest Has Been Given Away," is a beautiful melody for this dance. (*Note:* Originally, the dance was done only if the last child married was a girl, and only the mother was honored. Since parenting today is more of a joint responsibility, the tradition was altered to honor both parents when the last child, female or male, gets married.)

After-Dinner Grace

At the conclusion of the meal, the bride and groom approach the front of the room to cut the wedding cake. Photographs are taken, the first bite of cake is shared, and dessert and more dancing follow. Finally, the **Birkat Hamazon**, "Grace After the Meal," is chanted, followed by another recitation of the Sheva Berachot. It is customary to ask individual men who have not yet had the honor of participating in your *simcha* to now recite one of these blessings. Remember to assign the seventh blessing to one who is familiar with the melodies. After the Sheva Berachot are completed, the Ceremony of the Cups proceeds. One cup of wine represents the *Benchen* (Yiddish for "Grace"), and the other represents the Sheva Berachot. These two cups are poured into a third cup to combine the blessings. The wine is then poured back into the first two cups, and the bride and groom each drink from one of those two cups.

Ceremony of the Cups

At this time, if the American custom of throwing the bouquet is to be included, the band leader will call upon all the single women to join the bride at the front of the room. The bride then tosses the bouquet over her head to one lucky woman who receives the bride's good luck wishes and who, according to tradition, will be the next to wed. (Many brides order a special toss-away bouquet for this purpose so that they may keep their own bridal flowers.) The band leader may then call all the single men forward so the groom can toss the garter. The lucky man who catches the garter then places it on the leg of the woman who caught the bouquet, in hopes that they both will have the luck and good fortune to be the next ones married. Most Orthodox couples do not include these traditions, or have only the throwing of the bouquet, because of the rules of *tzniut*. In keeping with the American tradition, the couple leaves the reception in a shower of rice (to symbolize fertility), rose petals, confetti, or even a shimmering array of colored sequins.

Throwing the Bouquet

Tossing the Garter

AFTER THE WEDDING

Some couples choose to postpone their honeymoon until one week after their wedding in order to celebrate their first week with family and friends. This seven-day celebration is based on the biblical recounting of Jacob's week of celebrating after his marriage to Leah. Another explanation points out the significance of the comparison of one's wedding with one's death. Both of these two very emotional events require an adjustment period. As when one is "sitting *Shiva*," or mourning, the joy or sorrow is shared among family and friends for seven days to ease the individual burden. Also, the Shulchan Aruch states that when a man marries, he should *rejoice* with his bride for seven days; no work or business transactions should occur during this time, so that he may devote himself to her.

The First Week

Each day following the wedding, a *minyan* gathers in the morning and the evening (or just once a day) to say the Sheva Berachot again in honor of the bride and groom. (You are considered to be the bride and groom for one year's worth of celebrations and holidays, and *then* you are called wife and husband.) There should be a **panim chadashot**, a "new face," among the guests each day, to renew the rejoicing, except on the Shabbat because the Sabbath is "new" each week. (*Note*: If the bride and groom were both married, the Sheva Berachot are said only at the wedding.)

A New Face

Honeymoons are traditional and can take a myriad of shapes, which we will not discuss in this book as the information is readily available from family, friends, and travel agents. The interesting history dates back to that northern European "steal the bride" custom, after which the groom hid out with his bride for one month to let tempers settle. The newlyweds drank a sweet drink made from honey by the light of the moon. From these practices, the word *honeymoon* was coined.

The final significant event related to the wedding ceremony is the couple's entrance into their new home. The American groom may carry his bride over the threshold, often accompanied by real or feigned grunting and groaning. A Sephardic family in Israel may break a specially baked bread, *ruskah*, over the newlyweds' heads. Or, you may have an idea of your own!

OTHER JEWISH WEDDING TRADITIONS

Many old and beautiful Jewish traditions involve very little planning: you simply decide that you would like them included and so instruct your rabbi, caterer, or band leader. The easiest and one of the most meaningful traditions is the giving of **tzedakah**, charity, by the bride and groom. At this time of such joy, they should remember those who are less fortunate. An organization was developed in July 1985 as a response to the world hunger situation: **Mazon** ("sustenance" in Hebrew) is a group whose goal is to raise awareness among Jews about world hunger and to raise money for Jews and non-Jews worldwide. Mazon proposes that the family voluntarily impose a 3% tax on the "rites of passage" celebrations: Bar and Bat Mitzvahs and weddings. This figure was chosen because, based on the average $17,000 families are spending on these *simchas*, a $500 donation does not place too much additional strain on the budget. Contact your local rabbi for more information or call Mazon. (See section entitled "Other Things You Should Know" in the back of this book.)

Another important, respectful tradition is honoring the memory of one's parents if one or both parents are deceased. Before the wedding, the bride and/or groom should visit the parent's grave and recite the **Kaddish**, the Memorial Prayer. If it is impossible to go to the grave, the Memorial Prayer should be said in the synagogue on the Monday or Thursday before the wedding day.

One tradition which takes some advance planning is the groom's **Aufruf**, calling to the Torah before his marriage. Usually on the Shabbat before the wedding,* the groom is given an *aliyah* (called to the Torah), to be honored on his forthcoming marriage. He may also recite the *Haftorah*, a portion from the Prophets. (Although less common, an *Aufruf* can take place on a Monday or a Thursday, the other days when the Torah is read.) Other family members and close friends may also be honored by being given *aliyot* (plural). At the conclusion of the groom's *aliyah* or *maftir* (the last reading from the Torah on Shabbat morning), the rabbi blesses the bride and groom. In

---

*One tradition among some couples is to refrain from seeing each other for one week before the wedding in order to build up the anticipation and excitement of the wedding day. If observing this custom, plan the *Aufruf* on the Shabbat *one week* before the wedding, so that the bride may attend.

many synagogues, it is customary for the congregation to shower the groom with candy, nuts, or raisins. (Most synagogues allow this tradition only if the candy is wrapped in small, individual, sealed bags, thus preventing extensive cleanup. Tying them with ribbons in the colors chosen for the wedding makes them more festive.) The reason that nuts are thrown is that the numerical value of the letters in the Hebrew word for nut, *egoz*, add up to 17--the same numerical value of the letters in *tov*, the Hebrew word for "good." Candy and raisins symbolize a wish for a "sweet and fruitful life" for the bride and groom. Following services, the groom's family may sponsor a *kiddush*--refreshments such as wine and cake--for the congregation. As with most *simchas*, the family is encouraged to share its joy with the community.

The **mikvah**, ritual bath, is a special pool where ceremonial immersion, **tevilah**, takes place and the bride is purified before her wedding day. She should make her visit just before the wedding and at least seven days after menstruation stops. (Counting begins in the evening, as the Hebrew day lasts from nightfall to nightfall.) A bride may make an appointment to go to the *mikvah* before normal operating hours. In this way, she will receive special attention and guidance from the *mikvah* attendant, who will explain the entire procedure. First, all jewelry is removed and the bride will take a bath and then a shower and shampoo: the body must be completely clean. Next the attendant will perform a routine inspection. (Try not to be intimidated--she is only doing her job.) She will then instruct the bride on how to immerse her body in the pool so that the water reaches every nook and cranny. After she has said the appropriate blessings (the attendant will help her here, too), she leaves the *mikvah* area, gets dressed, and leaves a small contribution before returning home.

The Bath of Purification

Men may also visit the *mikvah* and are encouraged to do so. The groom should call in advance because the times when the *mikvah* is open for men are limited. Many Orthodox women and men continue going to the *mikvah* after they are married. For more information, contact your rabbi or the *mikvah* attendant.

UNUSUAL SITUATIONS

Let us take a brief moment to discuss some very unusual situations. If a member of the immediate family is very ill, the wedding should be postponed only if the patient requests it. If not, the wedding should continue as planned so that the ill person does not feel guilty for post-poning or lessening your joy. If there is a death in the immediate family, the wedding should be postponed at least until after the seven days of *Shiva* and preferably until after **Sheloshim**, the thirty days after burial. After *Sheloshim*, it is permitted to continue the festivities as planned--music, food, fancy clothing--without showing any signs of mourning. Finally, some marriages are not meant to be. If there is a broken engagement, guests should be notified by mail or telephone, and all gifts should be returned, including the engagement ring.

The beautiful Jewish and American traditions that have been described can add much meaning and joy to your wedding. If some are more attractive to you than others, by all means pick and choose those you like. Any customs or traditions that are chosen will flavor your day in a special way for you.

Now, on to the planning!

NOTES

SUMMARY OF JEWISH AND AMERICAN WEDDING TRADITIONS

Tradition	*Jewish or American*
The Wedding Day	
Fasting on the wedding day	Jewish
Bride's white gown	Both
Groom's *kittel*	Jewish
Before the Ceremony	
Kabbalat Panim/Chossen's Tish (Groom's Reception)	Jewish
Signing the *tena'im* (engagement contract)	Jewish
Breaking the plate	Jewish
Ketubbah (marriage contract)	Jewish
Kinyan (formal acceptance)	Jewish
Signing the *ketubbah*	Jewish
Attending the Bride	Jewish
Badeken die Kallah (Veiling of the Bride)	Jewish
Seating of guests--by ushers	American
Seating of guests--by themselves	Jewish
Processional and the *Chuppah*	
Attendants	Both
Processional	Both
Candles in processional	Jewish
Chuppah (wedding canopy)	Jewish
Stance under the *chuppah*	Jewish
The Ceremony	
Bride circling the groom	Jewish
Kiddushin/Erusin (Engagement Ceremony)	Jewish
Three Halachic requirements	Jewish
Marriage vows	Jewish
Double-ring ceremony	American
Reading of *ketubbah*	Jewish
Nissuin (Wedding Ceremony)	Jewish
Sheva Berachot (Seven Blessings)	Jewish
Drinking wine	Both
Official pronouncement	American
Breaking the glass	Jewish
The kiss	American
After the Ceremony	
Yichud (Seclusion)/*Bi'ah* (Cohabitation)	Jewish
Recessional	Both
Photography session	Jewish

The Reception

Introducing the couple	American
Circle dancing	Jewish
Motzi over *challah* (blessing over bread)	Jewish
Table photographs	Both
Toasts	Both
Tapping spoons on glasses	American
Reading telegrams	American
Mezinke Tanz (dance honoring the marriage of the last child in the family)	Jewish
Cutting the cake	American
Birkat Hamazon (Grace After the Meal)	Jewish
Ceremony of the cups	Jewish
Throwing the bouquet and/or garter	American
Leaving in shower of rice or rose petals	Both

After the Wedding

Sheva Berachot celebrations (first week)	Jewish
Honeymoon	American
Entering new home	Both

Other Jewish Wedding Traditions

Tzedakah (charity)	Jewish
Honoring memory of one's parents	Jewish
Groom's *Aufruf* (calling to the Torah before the wedding)	Jewish
Mikvah (ritual bath)	Jewish

NOTES

Part II

Getting Started

LET'S GET FOCUSED!

Projected budget: $_____

Approximate number of guests: _____

Kosher?   ☐ no ☐ yes   Glatt kosher? ☐ no ☐ yes

Jewish customs to be included (check those which apply):

☐ *Aufruf* (groom's calling to the Torah)
☐ *Mikvah* (ritual bath)
☐ *Ketubbah* (marriage contract)
☐ Fasting
☐ *Kabbalat Panim/Tena'im* (prewedding ceremonies)
☐ *Badeken die Kallah* (Veiling of the Bride)
☐ Candles (for processional)
☐ *Chuppah* (wedding canopy)
☐ *Kittel* (groom's white garment)
☐ Bride circling the groom
☐ Breaking the glass
☐ Separate seating (men and women):
    ☐ Ceremony
    ☐ Reception
☐ Separate dancing (men and women)
☐ Washing before *motzi:*
    ☐ Bride and groom
    ☐ All guests
☐ *Mezinke Tanz* (if last child being married)
☐ *Benchen* (Grace After the Meal)
☐ *Sheva Berachot* celebration(s) (the first week)
☐ Other _____

American customs to be included (check those which apply):

☐ Engagement party
☐ Bridal shower(s)
☐ Bridal party luncheon
☐ Rehearsal party or dinner
☐ Double-ring ceremony
☐ Throwing the bridal bouquet
☐ Tossing the garter
☐ Other _____

Your highest priorities (rank from 1 to 9, high to low):

_____ Officiant(s) (rabbi, cantor)
_____ Time of year, date, day of week
_____ Jewish customs (*Tena'im, Badeken,* synagogue, etc.)
_____ Caterer
_____ Music (ceremony, reception)
_____ Location (synagogue, catering hall, restaurant, gallery)
_____ Ambiance (flowers, attire, etc.)
_____ Tangible memories (photographs, video)
_____ Other _____

Choice of date: 1st _____ 2nd _____ 3rd _____

Choice of time: 1st _____ 2nd _____ 3rd _____

DATES TO AVOID

According to Jewish law, weddings are forbidden on these days:

- Rosh Hashanah (Jewish New Year)
- Yom Kippur (Day of Atonement)
- Sukkot (Tabernacles, Feast of Booths)
- Pesach (Passover)
- Shavuot (Pentecost)
- During the Counting of the Omer (the 7 weeks from Pesach to Shavuot, excluding Lag B'Omer, and, according to some, Yom Ha'atzma'ut [Israel's Independence Day] and Yom Yerushalayim [Jerusalem Reunification Day])
- The Three Weeks (from the seventeenth of Tammuz to the ninth of Av)
- Fast Days:
  Tisha B'Av
  Tenth of Tevet
  Seventeenth of Tammuz
  Fast of Gedaliah (third of Tishrei)
  Fast of Esther (third of Adar)

(*Note*: If time or financial restraints prohibit a weekend wedding, consider a weekday wedding. According to tradition, Tuesday is a good day because, during the week of creation, Tuesday was the only day on which God twice said, "*Ki tov,*" "It was good." Monday is a less favorable day for a wedding because God did not even once say, "It was good" on the second day of creation.)

FAMILY FACTS--BRIDE

Name _____
Address _____
City _____
State _____ Zip _____
Home phone _____
Car/Cellular phone/Pager _____

Work phone _____
E-mail address _____
Home Fax _____
Work Fax _____
Occupation _____
Best times to call _____

PARENTS

Name _____
Address _____
City _____
State _____ Zip _____
Home phone _____
Car/Cellular phone/Pager _____

Work phone _____
E-mail address _____
Home Fax _____
Work Fax _____
Occupation _____
Best times to call _____

Name _____
Address _____
City _____
State _____ Zip _____
Home phone _____
Car/Cellular phone/Pager _____

Work phone _____
E-mail address _____
Home Fax _____
Work Fax _____
Occupation _____
Best times to call _____

Siblings' Names _____

GRANDPARENTS

Name _____
Address _____
City _____
State _____ Zip _____
Home phone _____
Car/Cellular phone/Pager _____

Work phone _____
E-mail address _____
Home Fax _____
Work Fax _____
Occupation _____
Best times to call _____

Name _____
Address _____
City _____
State _____ Zip _____
Home phone _____
Car/Cellular phone/Pager _____

Work phone _____
E-mail address _____
Home Fax _____
Work Fax _____
Occupation _____
Best times to call _____

Name _____
Address _____
City _____
State _____ Zip _____
Home phone _____
Car/Cellular phone/Pager _____

Work phone _____
E-mail address _____
Home Fax _____
Work Fax _____
Occupation _____
Best times to call _____

Name _____
Address _____
City _____
State _____ Zip _____
Home phone _____
Car/Cellular phone/Pager _____

Work phone _____
E-mail address _____
Home Fax _____
Work Fax _____
Occupation _____
Best times to call _____

FAMILY FACTS--GROOM

Name _____   Work phone _____
Address _____   E-mail address _____
City _____   Home Fax _____
State _____ Zip _____   Work Fax _____
Home phone _____   Occupation _____
Car/Cellular phone/Pager _____ Best times to call _____

PARENTS

Name _____   Work phone _____
Address _____   E-mail address _____
City _____   Home Fax _____
State _____ Zip _____   Work Fax _____
Home phone _____   Occupation _____
Car/Cellular phone/Pager _____ Best times to call _____

Name _____   Work phone _____
Address _____   E-mail address _____
City _____   Home Fax _____
State _____ Zip _____   Work Fax _____
Home phone _____   Occupation _____
Car/Cellular phone/Pager _____ Best times to call _____
Siblings' Names _____

GRANDPARENTS

Name _____   Work phone _____
Address _____   E-mail address _____
City _____   Home Fax _____
State _____ Zip _____   Work Fax _____
Home phone _____   Occupation _____
Car/Cellular phone/Pager _____ Best times to call _____

Name _____   Work phone _____
Address _____   E-mail address _____
City _____   Home Fax _____
State _____ Zip _____   Work Fax _____
Home phone _____   Occupation _____
Car/Cellular phone/Pager _____ Best times to call _____

Name _____   Work phone _____
Address _____   E-mail address _____
City _____   Home Fax _____
State _____ Zip _____   Work Fax _____
Home phone _____   Occupation _____
Car/Cellular phone/Pager _____ Best times to call _____

Name _____   Work phone _____
Address _____   E-mail address _____
City _____   Home Fax _____
State _____ Zip _____   Work Fax _____
Home phone _____   Occupation _____
Car/Cellular phone/Pager _____ Best times to call _____

KETUBBAH INFORMATION SHEET

Ordering your *ketubbah* has its technicalities also! You can speed up the process by completing this information sheet before placing your order. The information must be checked by your rabbi and show his signature in order for the *sofer* (scribe) to begin the calligraphy. (The *sofer* may begin on the artwork before receiving this information.)

Person ordering *ketubbah* _____

Phone _____

Address _____

City/State/Zip _____

Ketubbah to be mailed to _____

Phone _____

Address _____

City/State/Zip _____

COMPLETE THE FOLLOWING IN HEBREW

Groom _____

Groom's father _____

Groom's mother _____

Groom's family name _____

Bride _____

Bride's father _____

Bride's mother _____

Bride's family name _____

Town or city where wedding will occur _____

State where wedding will occur _____

Date of wedding and time of day _____

Jewish year _____

Is either the bride's father or the groom's father a *Cohen* or a *Levite*?* ☐ no ☐ yes
Is either father deceased? ☐ no ☐ yes
Has either the bride or the groom been divorced or widowed?** ☐ no ☐ yes
Has either the bride or the groom converted to Judaism? ☐ no ☐ yes

There are several alternatives for the *sofer* when he or she writes the word *ve'kanina*, the last word completed at the signing of the *ketubbah* during the Kabbalat Panim, the groom's reception. Among them are leaving the entire word out, omitting one letter, or outlining the letters of the word. Inform your scribe of your decision before he or she begins on the calligraphy.

I have checked the preceding information and verify it as fact.

_____   _____
                        Rabbi   Date
*If one of the fathers is a Cohen or a Levite, then it is included as part of the name; e.g. Rochel Bat Moshe haCohen--Rachel, daughter of Moses, the Cohen. **A Cohen is prohibited from marrying a divorced person.

HOME WEDDINGS--SOME CONSIDERATIONS

Use worksheets provided if they apply to your situation. Other items to consider during the planning process include the following:

1. Where will the ceremony and reception be held in case of inclement weather? Do you need separate areas to be set up for the ceremony and reception? Never invite more people than you can accommodate indoors!

2. Do the following items have to be rented?

Buffet table(s)	Linens (tablecloths and napkins)
China	Outdoor placecards (to withstand wind)
Coat rack(s)	Outdoor restrooms
Dance floor	Portable bar(s)
Flatware	Serving pieces
Glassware	Sound system
Guest tables and chairs	Tent(s)

3. Will you need to hire waiters, waitresses, and/or bartenders?

4. Where will the guests park? Will you need to hire special police to direct traffic and/or valets to park cars?

5. Who will cater? Will the preparation be done in your kitchen? If you are cooking or baking, do you have enough freezer and refrigerator space?

6. Is there someone who will watch the house, answer phones, and direct guests before, during, and after the affair? Do you have a close friend or family member who will help with the final details in the last days before the wedding?

7. Where will coats be hung?

8. Are there enough bathroom facilities or will you need to rent a porta-john? Do you have a plumber on-call for an emergency?

9. Is there a private room in which the bride can get ready?

10. Are there enough electrical outlets? How many extension cords do you need? Do you have enough power supply to handle the extra capacity?

11. Does your homeowner's insurance cover any damages to or loss of property or gifts?

12. How much investment is necessary to straighten up and beautify the interior and exterior of your house, plus your garden and lawn?

13. How much investment will be required to restore your home and yard to their original state?

Having your wedding at home may not be less expensive than having it at a synagogue, catering hall, or elsewhere, but, if you have the time and patience, your wedding may well be more meaningful to you. Good luck!

WEDDING EXPENSES--WHAT TO EXPECT AND WHO PAYS

Listed below are the items on which you may spend money if you choose to include every tradition described in this book. Probably you will not have all of these expenses, but you should be prepared for those small items that (so mysteriously!) add up.

Traditionally, the bride's family pays for the entire wedding; today, however, certain expenses are often designated as the groom's and his family's responsibility. The standard division of expenses is given here, but each family will individually decide who pays for each item, as my family and my husband's family did. For example, my family paid for all the flowers, rather than dividing the expense up, as suggested here. One large cost my husband's family graciously offered (and was gratefully allowed) to absorb was the band's fees.

Today, many couples divide the expenses more evenly between the two families or the couple pays for the entire wedding themselves. The best thing is for both families to sit down together, as early as possible, and make their decisions.

In the following list, **B** = bride and/or her family, **G** = groom and/or his family, and ***** = either. *Note*: Attendants usually pay for their own outfits, whether purchased or rented.

What to Expect	*Who Pays*
Announcements	B
Aufruf (donation and *kiddush* following services)	G
Aufruf bags and ribbons (to toss at groom)	*
Bag with glass (for groom to break)	*
Basket of amenities for the ladies' and/or men's room(s)	B
Benchers (booklets containing Grace After the Meal)	B
Blood test (required in most states)	
Bride	B
Groom	G
Bridal party luncheon	B
Bride's attire (gown, veil, shoes, gloves, etc.)	B
Bride's memories book	B
Cake knife	*
Calligrapher (invitation addresses, place cards)	B
Candles and matches	*
Caterer (plus **mashgiach** fee, if charged)	B
China plate (for mothers to break)	*
Chuppah (handmade) and poles	*
Cocktail napkins	B
The Complete Jewish Wedding Planner	*
Embosser (or address labels)	B
Engagement gifts:	
Bride's ring	G
Groom's ring	B
Entertainment (miscellaneous)	*
Florist	
Personal flowers for bride; groom's parents, attendants, and grandparents	G
Personal flowers for groom; bride's parents, attendants, and grandparents	B
All other floral needs for ceremony, reception, and decorating	B
Gifts (wedding)	
Bride; groom's parents and attendants	G
Groom; bride's parents and attendants	B
Guest registry book	B
Honeymoon	G

Hotel accommodations	
Bride's family and attendants	B
Groom's family and attendants	G
Index cards (or preprinted set) and file box for recording gifts	B
Informal notes/thank-you notes	B
Invitations and response cards (and extra envelopes)	B
Ketubbah	G
Kippot (yarmulkes)	G
Kittel	G
Liquor, wine, and/or champagne (often included in catering costs)	B
Marriage license	G
Match packs	B
Mikvah fee or donation	
Bride	B
Groom	G
Money bag (for wedding checks)	*
Music	B
Officiants' fees: rabbi, cantor	G
Pens--colored (for addressing invitations, thank-you notes, and announcements)	B
Personal care--wedding day (hair, makeup, manicure--You only get married once!)	B
Photographer	B
Place cards (if not provided by your caterer)	B
Bag with glass (for groom to smash)	*
Preserving (gown, veil, bridal bouquet)	B
Program (of wedding ceremony)	*
Rehearsal party or dinner	G
Rental fees--ceremony and reception sites, extra rooms	B
Rice, rose petals, confetti (to toss as bride and groom leave)	*
Ring pillow(s)	B
Rings (wedding)	
Bride	G
Groom	B
Stamps (invitations, response cards, thank-you notes, announcements)	B
Toasting glasses for bride and groom	*
Transportation for wedding party	*
Trousseau	B
Tuxedo rental	G
Tzedakah (charity)	Both
Veil	B
Videographer	B
Wedding cake with ornament(s) (often included in catering costs)	B
Wedding/party favors	B
Wedding planner's fee	*

GRAND CHECKLIST

Here is the key to your wedding planning success! Follow this schedule as closely as possible, and you will have *every* detail accomplished by your wedding day. Check off each item (inside lefthand boxes) as you complete it, and watch the checkmarks accumulate (as the checks and dollars dwindle!).

AS SOON AS YOU GET ENGAGED

☐ 1. Discuss your budget and complete "Let's Get Focused!" and "Family Facts."

☐ 2. Select and coordinate your priorities.
    ☐ Day, date, and time
    ☐ Rabbi and cantor
    ☐ Ceremony site
    ☐ Reception site
    ☐ Caterer

☐ 3. Choose the other key services that *must* be contracted in advance. Remember to comparison-shop to get the best quality for the best price.
    ☐ Music
    ☐ Photographer
    ☐ Videographer
    ☐ Florist

☐ 4. Have engagement photos taken.

☐ 5. Pick up engagement photos, write engagement announcement, and send announcement and photo (name and address on back) to local newspapers. Most papers will return your photo if you enclose a stamped, self-addressed envelope. Look in the newspaper for sample texts, but *don't* agonize; editors will usually rewrite your copy in any case.

☐ 6. Arrange a meeting with your rabbi.

☐ 7. Contract a *ketubbah* writer.

☐ 8. Select a *ketubbah* design and place your order. Complete "*Ketubbah* Information Sheet." Send a copy to your rabbi for his signature and request that he send it directly to your artist.

☐ 9. Schedule and plan your engagement party.

☐ 10. Buy, address, and mail engagement party invitations. Remember to buy plenty of stamps.

PRIOR TO THREE MONTHS BEFORE THE WEDDING

☐ 11. Begin to assemble your guest lists for the wedding. Each family, as well as the bride and groom, should compile a separate list based on the previously agreed-upon amount of guests allotted for each family or person.

☐ 12. Buy a preprinted set of blank gift record cards or buy an appropriate number of 4 x 6-inch index cards and a file box. If you *do* buy the blank cards and plan to type them yourself, or have them printed locally, you should begin *now* on everything except the names and addresses because this is a large task in itself. Do not begin typing in the guest information yet because your lists will be subjected to major alterations, additions, and subtractions in the months to come--I speak from experience!

☐ 13. Choose your attendants--bride's and groom's--and invite them to participate.

☐ 14. Decide on your color scheme. Consider complexion and hair color of attendants and family, as well as the decor of the rooms you have reserved for your ceremony, reception, and picture taking (carpeting, walls, etc.).

☐ 15. Make a date with your fiancé to visit your favorite stores and register your gift choices. You might as well take the time now to give your guests ideas of what you like, rather than having to worry about duplicates and returns later. Celebrate your choices with an intimate lunch or dinner for two--by now, you really appreciate those precious few moments together!

☐ 16. Now that you have made some gift selections, adjust "Bride and Groom's Wish List" and complete "We Already Have" list of items you do not want duplicated. Give these lists, as well as the names of the stores where you have registered, to your mothers and maid or matron of honor. They will gladly spread the word!

☐ 17. If you are, or a friend is, planning to crochet *kippot* (*yarmulkes*) for the groom, fathers, grandfathers, and male attendants, you should choose the designs and buy the yarn in the colors that coordinate with the wedding colors. Begin crocheting now because this is a time-consuming and tedious project--but well worth the effort! (Or contract a craftsperson to create them.)

☐ 18. Begin shopping for bride's attire and accessories. You may find all these items at one or more bridal shops, or you may want to buy or order some of them from your stationer or party store.

☐ 19. Help your bridal party and mothers choose their dresses, or assign this task to your maid or matron of honor. This project can be a lot of fun or very frustrating. You can make the selection easier if you give all the attendants and mothers samples of fabric that resemble the colors and fabrics you have in mind. If you have found a dress that best illustrates your idea, the bridal shop will often cut a small piece from the sample card for you to show everyone. Do not expect perfection: colors are sometimes very difficult to match exactly. Remember to give color samples to the mother(s) of the flower girl(s) also.

☐ 20. Decide on the attire for the groom and his attendants. You may choose formal wear or business suits, but be sure that the groom stands out in his own outfit. A formal wear shop will discuss clothing etiquette with you, if you wish.

☐ 21. Begin searching for your new home and furniture, if necessary. Remember to ask family members for extra items they might have available to donate. You may be surprised at some of the beautiful pieces of furniture that have been stored away in attics or basements. Your first home together does not have to be totally coordinated or matched--it needs only to be cozy and have *shalom bayit,* "peace in the house." After all, you plan to be together a long time and will have ample opportunity to update.

☐ 22. Plan your honeymoon and make all reservations. You can easily enlist the services of a travel agent, but be sure that you make the final decisions regarding the itinerary and details. You certainly don't want any surprises! It is important that you make these arrangements months in advance, especially if you are getting married in the busiest months of the year: April, May, June, and September.

☐ 23. Begin to compile a list of music selections you would like to hear at the special moments during the ceremony and reception, as well as a list of those songs you would like as background or for dancing.

☐ 24. Schedule appointments with your doctors (physician, dentist, gynecologist, etc.). You want to start your new life together healthy!

☐ 25. Choose and contract other services to make your day very special.
    ☐ Calligrapher: for invitation addresses and place cards
    ☐ Transportation: for wedding party
    ☐ Miscellaneous expenses: balloons, personalized chocolates, etc.

☐ 26. Begin planning and shopping for your trousseau.

☐ 27. Schedule *Aufruf* for the groom with your rabbi. Remember to include a list of the names of other male relatives to be honored with *aliyot*, so the rabbi can make arrangements for them, too.

☐ 28. Continue working on your wedding guest list and preparing blank gift record cards.

☐ 29. Experiment with hairstyles and makeup, but avoid anything drastic! Your groom loves you the way you are!

☐ 30. Make an appointment for your blood tests, if required in your state. Try to go together--another excuse to see each other and have a small break from the family and planning!

☐ 31. Buy gifts for your attendants and parents. This relatively easy task can be accomplished now, when you have a little more time to find meaningful gifts, rather than waiting until the hectic weeks before the wedding.

☐ 32. Buy wedding gifts for each other. Unfortunately, this is not something you really want to do together unless you are getting each other "his and her" gifts. This gift should be very memorable and sturdy--you want it to last your whole lives, and longer!

☐ 33. Buy your wedding ring(s). Another chance to steal away with your honey! If you plan to have the rings engraved, you should buy or borrow a plain, unbroken band--maybe your parent's ring or an heirloom--for the ceremony. A gold coin, the original object exchanged during the marriage ceremony, may be used instead.

☐ 34. By now you should have decided which wedding dress (and some of the accessories) you want. Order or purchase your gown and schedule fittings. Again, if you are getting married during the busy season, it is *imperative* that your gown be ordered with plenty of lead time, just in case there is any problem with the manufacturer, fabric, fit, or shipping (all of which are *common* occurrences and can cause great trauma!).

☐ 35. Complete arrangements for your new home and any furnishings you expect to arrive before or after you get back from your honeymoon.

☐ 36. If you are creating your own *chuppah*, pick your design and begin working on it. You may want to buy the poles now, too. If you plan to have an original *chuppah*, it should be ordered now.

THREE MONTHS BEFORE THE WEDDING

☐ 37. Choose and order:

☐ Invitations, response cards, and envelopes: When you go to your printer, be sure to take a copy of your invitation and response card texts, if you can prepare them in advance. If the bride is retaining her maiden name, or if the couple is hyphenating their last names, you should also order cards to that effect to enclose with the invitations. (And don't forget directions and/or maps, if necessary.) Your stationer will help you with the special wording of the texts if there are any touchy family situations. You should take home an exact duplicate of the texts ordered, in case there is a problem.

It is a good idea to order twenty-five extra envelopes to allow for mistakes, and to request that they be shipped as soon as possible. "Drop shipment" means that they will be delivered to you, rather than to the stationer. Either method is worth the small extra charge because it enables you to begin addressing the envelopes as soon as they arrive.

☐ Thank-you notes with the bride's name only for acknowledging all engagement gifts, as well as early wedding gifts. Traditionally, the bride accepted and acknowledged *all* gifts, for herself and her fiancé/husband; today it is acceptable for wedding gift thank-you's to be in both names if written after the ceremony takes place.

☐ Thank-you notes with the *couple's* names.

☐ Announcements: These are sent to those family, friends, and business associates with whom you would like to share your good news even though they could not be invited to the wedding. They do not have to be addressed at this time because they do not get mailed until the day after the wedding.

☐ Directions and/or map: If these are to be printed, bring your text and/or a camera-ready map or drawing. These could simply be duplicated and cut at your local copy center.

☐ *Benchers*: These small booklets contain the *Birkat Hamazon* (Grace After the Meal). They are a beautiful memento of the wedding day, with your names and wedding date on the front. The fancier version includes many of the Hebrew melodies often sung before and/or after the *benchen*.

☐ *Kippot (yarmulkes):* If no one is crocheting *kippot* for the groom and attendants, you have the option of borrowing white ones from the synagogue or ordering plain or personalized ones from your stationer. *Kippot* can be obtained in a wide variety of styles, colors, and fabrics, such as velvet, suede, satin, leather, and taffeta. These personalized *kippot* also make a wonderful gift for the male guests of the wedding to take home and use for many years. Ask about matching bobby pins, too.

☐ Cocktail napkins: Usually used during the cocktail hour and for dessert--be sure to order enough.

☐ Place cards: These may be supplied to you by the caterer. If they are not, or if you do not like the ones provided, you have a wide selection from which to choose.

☐ Match packs: Remember--if you supply match packs, you encourage smoking.

☐ Wedding/party favors: Some couples order chocolates in a preprinted box. These are also available from a Kosher chocolatier.

☐ 38. Check your homeowner's insurance policy--does the floater cover your engagement ring and your forthcoming gifts? If not, take care of this immediately.

☐ 39. Buy the *kittel* for the groom.

☐ 40. Write and print up a wedding program, if you choose to give one out prior to the ceremony. This booklet explains the traditions that are being included before, during, and after the ceremony; and it serves as another memento of your *simcha*. (*Note*: The American wedding program lists the members of the wedding party and the names of the people reading any passages or poems included in the ceremony.)

☐ 41. Make a "Welcome" sign to place near the door where guests will arrive for the ceremony. It can be placed over the table on which you have your guest registry and programs. The sign should direct guests to the appropriate areas: coat room, Hachnasat Kallah (Attending the Bride), Kabbalat Panim (Groom's Reception), cocktail area, or directly to their seats for the ceremony.

☐ 42. Choose men for the honorary duties. In Orthodox tradition, these men must be *shomer* Shabbat and unrelated to the bride and groom and each other.

☐ 43. Confirm appointment for your final dress fitting. Remember to take your undergarments and shoes for the fitting.

☐ 44. Make sure you have spoken to your rabbi and are clear about the details of the ceremony. He will also be happy to answer any of your other questions at this time.

☐ 45. Be certain that all women (bridal attendants, mothers, grandmothers, and flower girls) have bought or ordered their dresses and have scheduled a formal fitting, if necessary. Confirm shoe color at this time, too. If shoes are being dyed, allow enough time and send an *actual swatch* from the dress!

☐ 46. Pick up change-of-address cards at the post office. Also, purchase postage stamps (in coordinating colors, if possible) for the outside envelopes of invitations, response card envelopes, thank-you notes, and announcements. Do you have your embosser or return address labels? Do you have your colored pens? Do your invitations require extra or overseas postage?

☐ 47. Use the diagram on page 7 and fill in the names of your family members, attendants, and officiants as they will appear standing under the *chuppah*. List the correct order for the processional and recessional. Make and distribute copies of this information to each person involved, including the band leader, photographer, videographer, and party planner. This will make the rehearsal much smoother.

☐ 48. If you are traveling out of the country on your honeymoon, you should make arrangements to obtain a passport, an international driver's license, and any necessary vaccinations/shots.

☐ 49. Arrange movement of your belongings to your new home. Confirm furniture deliveries, if applicable.

☐ 50. Confirm male attire with all men in the wedding party, as well as with the officiants. (They may be able to match clothing, too.) If the men are wearing formal wear, confirm arrival date and pickup dates several days before the wedding.

☐ 51. Arrange accommodations and transportation for out-of-town guests. Pay in advance, if possible.

☐ 52. Complete formal wedding guest list. Try to stay calm and schedule enough time so that you will not be rushed. This is one of the hardest jobs! (If you think this is hard, wait until you have to do the seating chart!!)

☐ 53. Invitations: Address, emboss, stamp, stuff, and seal. You will need invitations and enclosures, envelopes, embosser or address labels, stamps (outside envelopes and response card envelopes), directions and/or map, announcements regarding retention of maiden name or hyphenation of name, colored pens, sponge, and water. Consult your stationer for the proper stuffing procedure. (Six to eight weeks before the wedding is the appropriate time for mailing.)

☐ 54. Fill in the names and addresses of guests on gift record cards, which should already be in a file box. There should be one card for each person or family to which you sent an invitation. File the cards alphabetically or by family, whichever is easier for you.

☐ 55. Give your completed music selections list to the band leader.

☐ 56. Arrange for all insurance policies to include you and your future spouse as of your wedding day:
    ☐ Health
    ☐ Auto
    ☐ Homeowner's
    ☐ Life

☐ 57. Buy any other small items (i.e., your guest registry book and a fancy feathered pen) and gifts which you do not yet have.

SIX WEEKS UNTIL WEDDING DAY

☐ 58. Mail invitations. Check postage for any invitations being mailed out of the country.

☐ 59. Reserve any rental equipment.

☐ 60. You might want to give the "Bridal Shower Guest List" to a family member. It will save her time trying to construct her own list, if she is planning to give you a bridal shower.

☐ 61. Give some *tzedakah* (charity) now. A small donation by each of you is a wonderful way to share your joy with those less fortunate. If you plan to give to *Mazon*, you may wait until after the *simcha*, at which time you will know your total expenditures, so that you can calculate your 3% donation.

☐ 62. Complete your list of people to whom you will mail a wedding announcement. Address and stamp these envelopes to be mailed the day after the wedding.

ONE MONTH UNTIL WEDDING DAY!

☐ 63. Set up all appointments to pamper yourself for the wedding day. (See Bride's Personal Care.)

☐ 64. Begin writing thank-you notes--a few each day is easier than dozens after the honeymoon! Remember to keep track of each gift on your gift record cards.

☐ 65. Order all your floral needs and any other accessories supplied by the florist.

☐ 66. Order liquor, wine, and/or champagne, if not included in the catering contract.

☐ 67. Order wedding cake, if not included in the catering contract. Be sure to specify which cake ornament you would prefer; you may want to confirm the hair color of the ornament's bride and groom, so they resemble the two of you, or get the ornament early and paint it to match. You may also want to paint a *kippah* on the head of the groom on the ornament. Or you can order something unique from a specialty house. My cousin used a black enamel kitten couple on top of her wedding cake.

☐ 68. Complete your photographic schedule (poses, people, times, places). Make copies and distribute to all people involved, especially the photographer!

☐ 69. Arrange to get foreign car insurance (if you are traveling abroad) from your insurance company.

☐ 70. Wrap all gifts. (If you don't have them yet, *hurry up!*)

☐ 71. Plan and schedule rehearsal party or dinner for a few days before the wedding. Compile guest list and call everyone with the relevant details.

☐ 72. Confirm *Aufruf* details with the rabbi and give him the English and Hebrew names of the groom and all other men who will have *aliyot*.

☐ 73. Have you seen all of your doctors? Do you need extra vitamins for the next month?

☐ 74. Have you had your blood tests, if required in your state? Do you have the results?

☐ 75. Apply for your marriage license. Take the original copy of the blood test (save a copy for yourself) and the fee. (Check with the marriage license office of your local government for the amount.) Processing usually takes twenty-four to forty-eight hours.

☐ 76. Pick up your marriage license. It *is* really happening!

☐ 77. Choose final menu and confirm with the caterer.

☐ 78. Complete your trousseau. Hang clothes in the closet to prevent wrinkling.

☐ 79. Confirm reservations for out-of-town guests. Pay now if you haven't already.

☐ 80. Confirm completion of *kippot* and *chuppah* if they are being created by hand.

☐ 81. Call relatives and friends to invite them to the groom's *Aufruf*.

☐ 82. Arrange for a friend or relative to take care of small children if they get unruly at any time during the affair.

ONLY TWO WEEKS LEFT!

☐ 83. Give the final guest count to the caterer. (All responses should have been received by now. If not, make a few phone calls--occasionally an invitation really does get lost in the mail.) It is better to give the caterer a *lesser* number of guests--you can always pay for the extra people the day of the affair, but it is difficult to get a refund. Remember: a small percentage of *confirmed* guests will not make it to the reception.

☐ 84. Make up seating chart. (The caterer will usually give you a diagram to fill in.) Keep in mind family and friends who do not get along. It is a nice idea to mix the two families at each table; this gives them a chance to meet each other, as well as to make some new friends. You never know what will result from a mixed table of single friends and relatives!

☐ 85. Write (or have your calligrapher letter) the guests' names on the place cards. Alphabetize the cards and put them in a box, ready to give to the caterer (who will line them up on the table outside the reception hall).

☐ 86. Confirm *all* details. The easiest way to do this is to refer to the section headed "Wedding Expenses--What to Expect and Who Pays." Be certain that all plans are correct according to your wishes and the contract. Any changes you want to make must be done now.

☐ 87. Pick up *ketubbah* (unless it is being mailed to you). This should be done by the groom if he is not showing the finished product to the bride until he gives it to her at the ceremony. (I found that the suspense was agony, but the *ketubbah* my father-in-law created was well worth the wait--it is a masterpiece!)

☐ 88. Give the original marriage license (keep a copy for yourself, just in case) to the rabbi. (Make sure that he has the *tena'im* paper, if you are including this ceremony.) Check all names, Hebrew and English.

☐ 89. Plan a luncheon or informal party for your bridal attendants. This gives you a chance to spend some time with the female family or friends who have been so helpful thus far. You can give them a small gift now or wait until the reception.

☐ 90. Pack all your belongings that are getting moved to your new home. Confirm details with movers.

☐ 91. Keep writing thank-you notes. You will be much happier later if you don't put this off!

☐ 92. Arrange any Sheva Berachot celebrations for the week after the wedding. These are often given by a relative, grandparents, or parents. Guests can include those already invited to the wedding reception and/or family, friends, and business associates whom you could not include or who could not come to the wedding. This gives them a chance to share your *simcha*. (Some even bring gifts!) Try to include a *panim chadashot*, "a new face," each night.

One Week Until Wedding Day!

☐ 93. Take some time now to honor the memory of your parent(s), if applicable. Go to the grave of any parent who might have passed away and recite *Kaddish*, the Memorial Prayer. If it is impossible to visit the grave, you should go to the synagogue on Monday or Thursday of this week and say the Memorial Prayer then.

☐ 94. Go to the bank to get cash for tips. Make sure that your account has enough money in it to cover the checks due on the wedding day. Think only of the beautiful memories this *simcha* will provide you for years to come!

☐ 95. Check to make sure that the gas, electricity, water, and telephone will be turned on in your new home a few days before you will move in.

☐ 96. Pack your wedding day toiletries bag.

☐ 97. Prepare a basket of amenities for the ladies' room similar to your wedding day toiletries bag. You may wish to place a small basket in the men's room, as well. Your guests will appreciate this added touch. Arrange for someone to pick up the remaining items and the basket(s) at the end of the day.

☐ 98. Are you at least trying to *relax*?!? Don't skip your regular exercise routine--it alleviates tensions and keeps your muscles strong for the big day ahead.

☐ 99. Begin packing for wedding night and honeymoon, if you are leaving for the honeymoon immediately after the wedding.

☐ 100. Eat a few balanced meals this week--you need your energy!

☐ 101. Make an appointment to go to the *mikvah*. Don't forget to take cash or a check for the fee or donation.

TWO DAYS TO GO!

☐ 102. Try on your clothes for the honeymoon. Take care of any last-minute alterations--many brides lose a few pounds from their hectic pre-wedding pace. (We won't even discuss the opposite!) Pack, if you are leaving the day of, or the day after, the wedding. Otherwise, wait until a few days before your departure to avoid wrinkled clothes.

☐ 103. Arrange with your mother or maid/matron of honor to take care of preserving your gown, veil, and/or your bridal bouquet, as well as mailing your announcements. That's what they are there for!

☐ 104. Give the caterer the *final* count. (Remember to underestimate by one or two if anyone is "iffy" at this point.)

YOU ARE GETTING MARRIED TOMORROW!

☐ 105. Set out all the items needed for tomorrow. (See "Items That Go To The Ceremony And Reception Sites.")

☐ 106. Do whatever you can to relax: a bubble bath, a massage, a ten-mile jog!

☐ 107. If the wedding is in the morning, set your alarm clock and arrange for a backup. Allow plenty of time--you do not want to be rushed tomorrow. Nor do you want to be late!!

TODAY IS THE DAY!!!

☐ 108. Check your list to be sure that you have not forgotten anything. (Okay, have someone else check it if you are *that* nervous!)

☐ 109. Off you go! Have a great time, smile, and try to relax!

Mazel Tov! מזל טוב Bonne Chance! Felicidad! Congratulations!

THE DAY AFTER THE BIG DAY

(Have your mother or maid/matron of honor take care of these items. It's your time to really relax and enjoy now!)

☐ 110. Freeze the top layer of the wedding cake. It will be a very memorable addition to the first anniversary celebration a year from now. Did you save some cocktail napkins, too?

☐ 111. Take gown, veil, and/or ring pillow(s) to be preserved. Make sure the cleaner is reputable and professional. A well-preserved gown can make big dreams for little girls come true--my mother's gown, crinoline, and ring pillow made mine!

☐ 112. Take the bridal bouquet to be preserved.

☐ 113. Mail announcements and completed change-of-address cards.

☐ 114. Make sure all bills have been paid or due dates are confirmed.

☐ 115. If you will be making a donation to *Mazon*, leave a note for the bride, groom, and their families to take care of this immediately after the honeymoon.

☐ 116. Leave the bride a reminder to arrange her name change if she has taken the groom's last name or the couple has decided to hyphenate their last names.

☐ 117. Take any personal film to be developed. These will be the first photos available since professional proofs take months.

☐ 118. Confirm details for any Sheva Berachot celebrations.

☐ 119. Send the honeymooners off with lots of hugs and kisses. (A few tears are okay, too!)

☐ 120. Now sit back, relax, and treasure your memories!

You did a great job! You deserve to be very proud and happy!

Part III

Expense Worksheets

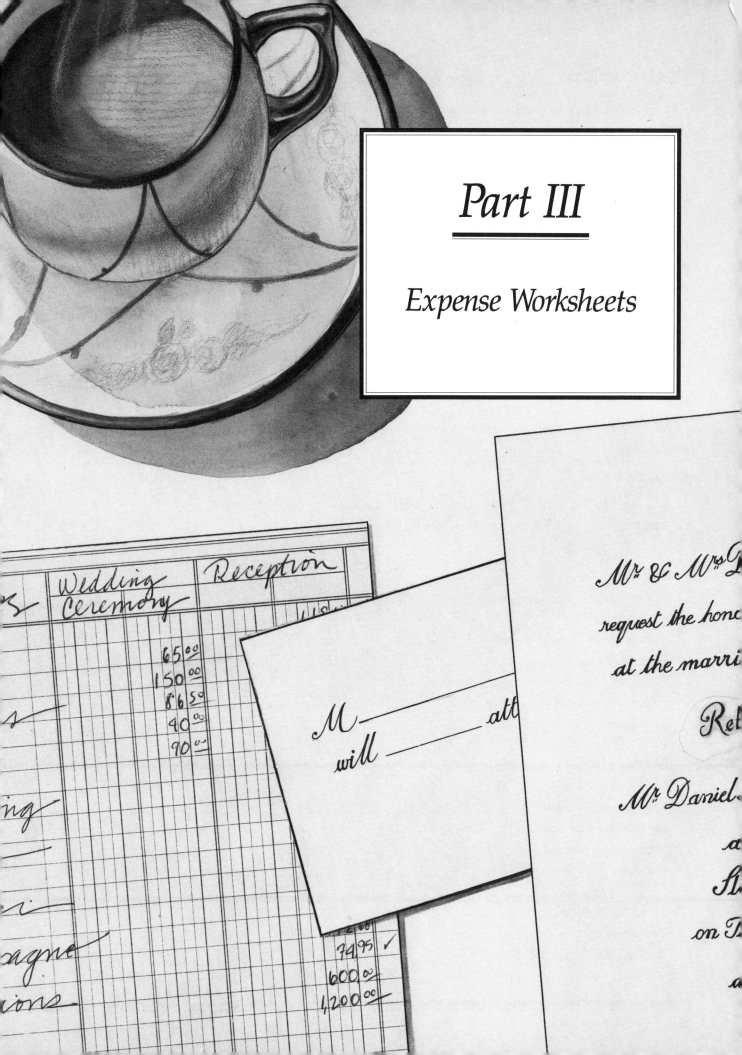

CEREMONY SITE

Name _____ Hours _____

Address _____ Phone _____

City _____ Fax _____

State _____ Zip _____ E-mail address _____

Contact _____ Internet _____

Rabbi _____ Cantor _____

Address _____ Address _____

City _____ City _____

State _____ Zip _____ State _____ Zip _____

Phone: Home _____ Phone: Home _____

      Work _____   Work _____

      Emergency _____   Emergency _____

Fax: Home _____ Fax: Home _____

      Work _____   Work _____

E-mail address _____ E-mail address _____

BASE FEE

$_____ (* = extra cost)

Guaranteed price? yes ☐ no ☐   Cost-of-living increase $ _____ or _____ %

INCLUDES

☐ Room _____

☐ *Chuppah*

☐ Bride's room _____

☐ Groom's room _____

☐ Changing room(s) for out-of-town guests _____

☐ Area or room for *Kabbalat Panim* _____

    ☐ Table

    ☐ Chairs

    ☐ Tablecloth

    ☐ Paper goods (napkins, cups)

☐ Area or hall for *Badeken* _____

    ☐ *Badeken* chair

☐ White *kippot* (*yarmulkes*)

☐ Room for pictures _____

    ☐ Color of walls _____

    ☐ Color of floor _____

☐ Coat room check

☐ Accessible to handicapped

Special regulations regarding lights, photographs, video, rice, etc. _____
_____
_____

Type of insurance carried _____
Cancellation policy _____
Date of ceremony _____ Time when rooms will be available _____
Total   = $ _____
Deposit paid on _____   =   _____
Balance due on _____   = $ _____

CEREMONY SITE

Name _____   Hours _____
Address _____   Phone _____
City _____   Fax _____
State _____ Zip _____   E-mail address _____
Contact _____   Internet _____

Rabbi _____   Cantor _____
Address _____   Address _____
City _____   City _____
State _____ Zip _____   State _____ Zip _____
Phone: Home _____   Phone: Home _____
     Work _____   Work _____
     Emergency _____   Emergency _____
Fax: Home _____   Fax: Home _____
     Work _____   Work _____
E-mail address _____   E-mail address _____

BASE FEE

$ _____ (* = extra cost)

Guaranteed price? ☐ yes ☐ no   Cost-of-living increase $ _____ or _____ %

INCLUDES

☐ Room _____
☐ *Chuppah*
☐ Bride's room _____
☐ Groom's room _____
☐ Changing room(s) for out-of-town guests _____
☐ Area or room for *Kabbalat Panim* _____
    ☐ Table
    ☐ Chairs

- ☐ Tablecloth
- ☐ Paper goods (napkins, cups)
☐ Area or hall for *Badeken* _____
- ☐ *Badeken* chair
☐ White *kippot* (*yarmulkes*)
☐ Room for pictures _____
- ☐ Color of walls _____
- ☐ Color of floor _____
☐ Coat room check
☐ Accessible to handicapped

Special regulations regarding lights, photographs, video, rice, etc. _____

_____

_____

Type of insurance carried _____

Cancellation policy _____

Date of ceremony _____ Time when rooms will be available _____

Total   = $ _____

Deposit paid on _____   =   _____

Balance due on _____   = $ _____

CEREMONY SITE

Name _____	Hours _____
Address _____	Phone _____
City _____	Fax _____
State _____ Zip _____	E-mail address _____
Contact _____	Internet _____

Rabbi _____	Cantor _____
Address _____	Address _____
City _____	City _____
State _____ Zip _____	State _____ Zip _____
Phone: Home _____	Phone: Home _____
Work _____	Work _____
Emergency _____	Emergency _____
Fax: Home _____	Fax: Home _____
Work _____	Work _____
E-mail address _____	E-mail address _____

BASE FEE

$ _____ (* = extra cost)

Guaranteed price? ☐ yes ☐ no   Cost-of-living increase $ _____ or _____ %

INCLUDES

☐ Room _____

☐ *Chuppah*

☐ Bride's room _____

☐ Groom's room _____

☐ Changing room(s) for out-of-town guests _____

☐ Area or room for *Kabbalat Panim* _____
    ☐ Table
    ☐ Chairs
    ☐ Tablecloth
    ☐ Paper goods (napkins, cups)

☐ Area or hall for *Badeken* _____
    ☐ *Badeken* chair

☐ White *kippot* (*yarmulkes*)

☐ Room for pictures _____
    ☐ Color of walls _____
    ☐ Color of floor _____

☐ Coat room check

☐ Accessible to handicapped

Special regulations regarding lights, photographs, video, rice, etc. _____

_____

_____

Type of insurance carried _____

Cancellation policy _____

Date of ceremony _____   Time when rooms will be available _____

Total   = $ _____

Deposit paid on _____   = _____

Balance due on _____   = $ _____

Reception Site and Caterer

Site

Name _____   Hours _____

Address _____   Phone _____

City _____   Fax _____

State _____ Zip _____   E-mail address _____

Contact _____   Internet _____

Included in Reception Room Charge: (* = extra charge)

☐ Tables: shape _____ size _____

☐ Chairs

☐ Cake table

☐ Piano

☐ Dance floor

☐ Coat room check

☐ Ladies' room attendant

☐ Parking: valet? ☐ yes ☐ no

Miscellaneous:

Type of insurance carried _____

Main decor colors _____

Other affairs on the same day?   ☐ yes ☐ no

Other affairs at the same time? ☐ yes ☐ no

Cancellation policy _____

Guaranteed price? ☐ yes ☐ no   Cost-of-living increase $ _____ or _____ %

Total   = $ _____

Deposit paid on _____   = _____

Balance due on _____   = $ _____

CATERER

Name _____

Address _____

City _____

State _____ Zip _____

Contact _____

On-site contact _____

Hours _____

Phone _____

Fax _____

E-mail address _____

Internet _____

Kosher? ☐ yes ☐ no   Glatt kosher? ☐ yes ☐ no

COST PER PERSON INCLUDES: (* = extra charge)

Guaranteed price? ☐ yes ☐ no   Cost-of-living increase $ _____ or _____ %

☐ Bar setup and mixes: hours _____ size _____

☐ Hors d'oeuvres: number _____

☐ *Challah* for *motzi*

☐ Soup

☐ Salad

☐ Main dish

☐ Buffet: captain-served? ☐ yes ☐ no

☐ Vegetables: number _____

☐ Rolls and butter or margarine

☐ Dessert: number _____

☐ Coffee and tea service

☐ Wedding cake: number of layers _____

                       flavor(s) _____

☐ Wedding cake ornament

☐ Wedding cake service (if not included, fee $ _____)

☐ Linens:

   ☐ Tablecloth(s): floor-length ☐ yes ☐ no

               colored

               round or square

☐ Napkins: colors _____

               fabric _____

☐ Place cards: quantity _____

☐ Type of service: ☐ waiters and/or waitresses: number _____

                ☐ French service*

                ☐ White glove service**

                ☐ Sommelier***

* " French service" means each item is served individually to the guest's plate.

** " White glove service" requires waiters and waitresses to wear white gloves when serving.

*** A "Sommelier" is a wine waiter who offers guests the opportunity to select his/her wine.

continued

☐ Floral centerpieces? _____

☐ Kitchen fee (if not included, fee = $ _____)

☐ *Mashgiach* fee (if not included, fee = $ _____)

☐ *Tena'im* refreshments (*kichel* [egg cookies], beverages)

What happens to leftovers? _____

Type of insurance carried _____

Cancellation policy _____

Cost: *Number*

Price per adult $ _____ x _____ = $ _____

    Child (aged _____ to _____) $ _____ x _____ = _____

    Service person (i.e., band) $ _____ x _____ = _____

Subtotal   _____ = $ _____

    Sales tax @ _____ %   = _____

    Gratuities @ _____ %   = _____

    Total   = $ _____

    Deposit paid on _____   = _____

    Balance due on _____   = $ _____

Arrival time _____ Place _____

RECEPTION SITE AND CATERER

SITE

Name _____   Hours _____

Address _____   Phone _____

City _____   Fax _____

State _____ Zip _____   E-mail address _____

Contact _____   Internet _____

INCLUDED IN RECEPTION ROOM CHARGE: (* = extra charge)

☐ Tables: shape _____ size _____

☐ Chairs

☐ Cake table

☐ Piano

☐ Dance floor

☐ Coat room check

☐ Ladies' room attendant

☐ Parking: valet? ☐ yes ☐ no

Miscellaneous:

Type of insurance carried _____

Main decor colors _____

Other affairs on the same day?   ☐ yes ☐ no

Other affairs at the same time? ☐ yes ☐ no

Cancellation policy _____

Guaranteed price? ☐ yes ☐ no   Cost-of-living increase $ _____ or _____ %

Total   = $ _____

Deposit paid on _____   =   _____

Balance due on _____   = $ _____

CATERER

Name _____

Address _____

City _____

State _____ Zip _____

Contact _____

On-site contact _____

Hours _____

Phone _____

Fax _____

E-mail address _____

Internet _____

Kosher? ☐ yes ☐ no   Glatt kosher? ☐ yes ☐ no

COST PER PERSON INCLUDES: (* = extra charge)

Guaranteed price? ☐ yes ☐ no   Cost-of-living increase $ _____ or _____ %

☐ Bar setup and mixes: hours _____ size _____

☐ Hors d'oeuvres: number _____

☐ *Challah* for *motzi*

☐ Soup

☐ Salad

☐ Main dish

☐ Buffet: captain-served? ☐ yes ☐ no

☐ Vegetables: number _____

☐ Rolls and butter or margarine

☐ Dessert: number _____

☐ Coffee and tea service

☐ Wedding cake: number of layers _____

                   flavor(s) _____

☐ Wedding cake ornament

☐ Wedding cake service (if not included, fee $ _____)

☐ Linens:

   ☐ Tablecloth(s): floor-length ☐ yes ☐ no

                colored

                round or square

☐ Napkins: colors _____

            fabric _____

☐ Place cards: quantity _____

☐ Type of service: ☐ waiters and/or waitresses: number _____

                   ☐ French service*

                   ☐ White glove service**

                   ☐ Sommelier***

*   " French service" means each item is served individually to the guest's plate.

**   " White glove service" requires waiters and waitresses to wear white gloves when serving.

***   A "Sommelier" is a wine waiter who offers guests the opportunity to select his/her wine.

continued

☐ Floral centerpieces? _____

☐ Kitchen fee (if not included, fee = $ _____)

☐ *Mashgiach* fee (if not included, fee = $ _____)

☐ *Tena'im* refreshments (*kichel* [egg cookies], beverages)

What happens to leftovers? _____

Type of insurance carried _____

Cancellation policy _____

Cost: *Number*

Price per adult $ _____ x _____ = $ _____

    Child (aged _____ to _____) $ _____ x _____ = _____

    Service person (i.e., band) $ _____ x _____ = _____

Subtotal   _____ = $ _____

    Sales tax @ _____ %   = _____

    Gratuities @ _____ %   = _____

    Total   = $ _____

    Deposit paid on _____   = _____

    Balance due on _____   = $ _____

Arrival time _____ Place _____

RECEPTION SITE AND CATERER

SITE

Name _____   Hours _____

Address _____   Phone _____

City _____   Fax _____

State _____ Zip _____   E-mail address _____

Contact _____   Internet _____

INCLUDED IN RECEPTION ROOM CHARGE: (* = extra charge)

☐ Tables: shape _____ size _____

☐ Chairs

☐ Cake table

☐ Piano

☐ Dance floor

☐ Coat room check

☐ Ladies' room attendant

☐ Parking: valet? ☐ yes ☐ no

Miscellaneous:

Type of insurance carried _____

Main decor colors _____

Other affairs on the same day?   ☐ yes ☐ no

Other affairs at the same time? ☐ yes ☐ no

Cancellation policy _____

Guaranteed price? ☐ yes ☐ no   Cost-of-living increase $ _____ or _____ %

Total   = $ _____

Deposit paid on _____   =   _____

Balance due on _____   = $ _____

CATERER

Name _____   Hours _____

Address _____   Phone _____

City _____   Fax _____

State _____ Zip _____   E-mail address _____

Contact _____   Internet _____

On-site contact _____

Kosher? ☐ yes ☐ no   Glatt kosher? ☐ yes ☐ no

COST PER PERSON INCLUDES: (* = extra charge)

Guaranteed price? ☐ yes ☐ no   Cost-of-living increase $ _____ or _____ %

☐ Bar setup and mixes: hours _____ size _____

☐ Hors d'oeuvres: number _____

☐ *Challah* for *motzi*

☐ Soup

☐ Salad

☐ Main dish

☐ Buffet: captain-served? ☐ yes ☐ no

☐ Vegetables: number _____

☐ Rolls and butter or margarine

☐ Dessert: number _____

☐ Coffee and tea service

☐ Wedding cake: number of layers _____

              flavor(s) _____

☐ Wedding cake ornament

☐ Wedding cake service (if not included, fee $ _____)

☐ Linens:

    ☐ Tablecloth(s): floor-length ☐ yes ☐ no

              colored

              round or square

☐ Napkins: colors _____

          fabric _____

☐ Place cards: quantity _____

☐ Type of service: ☐ waiters and/or waitresses: number _____

              ☐ French service*

              ☐ White glove service**

              ☐ Sommelier***

*   " French service" means each item is served individually to the guest's plate.

** " White glove service" requires waiters and waitresses to wear white gloves when serving.

*** A "Sommelier" is a wine waiter who offers guests the opportunity to select his/her wine.

continued

☐ Floral centerpieces? _____

☐ Kitchen fee (if not included, fee = $ _____)

☐ *Mashgiach* fee (if not included, fee = $ _____)

☐ *Tena'im* refreshments (*kichel* [egg cookies], beverages)

What happens to leftovers? _____

Type of insurance carried _____

Cancellation policy _____

Cost: *Number*

Price per adult $ _____ x _____ = $ _____

   Child (aged _____ to _____) $ _____ x _____ = _____

   Service person (i.e., band) $ _____ x _____ = _____

Subtotal   _____ = $ _____

   Sales tax @ _____ %   = _____

   Gratuities @ _____ %   = _____

   Total   = $ _____

   Deposit paid on _____   = _____

   Balance due on _____   = $ _____

Arrival time _____ Place _____

BAKERY

(Wedding cake may be included in the catering costs.)

Name _____   Hours _____

Address _____   Phone _____

City _____   Fax _____

State _____ Zip _____   E-mail address _____

Contact _____   Internet _____

COST INCLUDES: (* = extra charge)

Number of tiers _____

Cake flavor(s) _____

Icing flavor(s) _____

Icing color(s) _____

Ornament(s)--description _____

Design of cake _____

Subtotal   = $ _____

Delivery charge   =   _____

Sales tax   =   _____

Total   = $ _____

Deposit paid on _____   =   _____

Balance due on _____   = $ _____

BAKERY

(Wedding cake may be included in the catering costs.)

Name _____	Hours _____
Address _____	Phone _____
City _____	Fax _____
State _____ Zip _____	E-mail address _____
Contact _____	Internet _____

COST INCLUDES: (* = extra charge)

Number of tiers _____

Cake flavor(s) _____

Icing flavor(s) _____

Icing color(s) _____

Ornament(s)--description _____

Design of cake _____

Subtotal	=	$ _____
Delivery charge	=	_____
Sales tax	=	_____
Total	=	$ _____
Deposit paid on _____	=	_____
Balance due on _____	=	$ _____

MUSIC
(Band, strolling musicians, disc jockey, soloist, etc.)

Name _____   Type _____

Address _____   Hours _____

City _____   Phone _____

State _____ Zip _____   Fax _____

Contact _____   E-mail address _____

                                 Internet _____

FEE INCLUDES: (* = extra charge)

Guaranteed price? ☐ yes ☐ no   Cost-of-living increase $ _____ or _____ %

Badeken (background music)

    Number of musicians _____

    Playing time _____

    Instruments _____

Ceremony (processional, ceremony, recessional)

    Number of musicians _____

    Playing time _____

    Instruments _____

Cocktail reception

    Number of musicians _____

    Playing time _____   Continuous? ☐ yes ☐ no

    Instruments _____

Reception

    Number of musicians _____

    Playing time _____   Continuous? ☐ yes ☐ no

    Instruments _____

    Name of band _____

    Will you guarantee the band members in writing? ☐ yes ☐ no

    Can you provide a song list? ☐ yes ☐ no   Do you play requests? ☐ yes ☐ no

Type of insurance carried _____

Cancellation policy _____

Base charge   = $ _____

Overtime $ _____ per half hour per band member x _____   = _____

Total   = $ _____

Deposit paid on _____   = _____

Balance due on _____   = $ _____

Arrival Time _____ Place _____

MUSIC
(Band, strolling musicians, disc jockey, soloist, etc.)

Name _____   Type _____

Address _____   Hours _____

City _____   Phone _____

State _____ Zip _____   Fax _____

Contact _____   E-mail address _____

                                  Internet _____

FEE INCLUDES: (* = extra charge)

Guaranteed price? ☐ yes ☐ no   Cost-of-living increase $ _____ or _____ %

Badeken (background music)

    Number of musicians _____

    Playing time _____

    Instruments _____

Ceremony (processional, ceremony, recessional)

    Number of musicians _____

    Playing time _____

    Instruments _____

Cocktail reception

    Number of musicians _____

    Playing time _____   Continuous? ☐ yes ☐ no

    Instruments _____

Reception

    Number of musicians _____

    Playing time _____   Continuous? ☐ yes ☐ no

    Instruments _____

    Name of band _____

    Will you guarantee the band members in writing? ☐ yes ☐ no

    Can you provide a song list? ☐ yes ☐ no   Do you play requests? ☐ yes ☐ no

Type of insurance carried _____

Cancellation policy _____

Base charge   = $ _____

Overtime $ _____ per half hour per band member x _____   =   _____

Total   = $ _____

Deposit paid on _____   =   _____

Balance due on _____   = $ _____

Arrival Time _____ Place _____

MUSIC
(Band, strolling musicians, disc jockey, soloist, etc.)

Name _____   Type _____

Address _____   Hours _____

City _____   Phone _____

State _____ Zip _____   Fax _____

Contact _____   E-mail address _____

                                                      Internet _____

FEE INCLUDES: (* = extra charge)

Guaranteed price? ☐ yes ☐ no   Cost-of-living increase $ _____ or _____ %

Badeken (background music)

    Number of musicians _____

    Playing time _____

    Instruments _____

Ceremony (processional, ceremony, recessional)

    Number of musicians _____

    Playing time _____

    Instruments _____

Cocktail reception

    Number of musicians _____

    Playing time _____   Continuous? ☐ yes ☐ no

    Instruments _____

Reception

    Number of musicians _____

    Playing time _____   Continuous? ☐ yes ☐ no

    Instruments _____

    Name of band _____

    Will you guarantee the band members in writing? ☐ yes ☐ no

    Can you provide a song list? ☐ yes ☐ no   Do you play requests? ☐ yes ☐ no

Type of insurance carried _____

Cancellation policy _____

Base charge   = $ _____

Overtime $ _____ per half hour per band member x _____   =   _____

Total   = $ _____

Deposit paid on _____   =   _____

Balance due on _____   = $ _____

Arrival Time _____ Place _____

PHOTOGRAPHER

Name _____   Hours _____

Address _____   Phone _____

City _____   Fax _____

State _____ Zip _____   E-mail address _____

Contact _____   Internet _____

CONTRACTED FEE INCLUDES:

☐ Engagement pictures: number _____ Couple keeps proofs? ☐ yes ☐ no

☐ Hours at wedding _____

☐ Approximate number of pictures taken at wedding _____

☐ Proof album

☐ Negatives available until _____

☐ Bride and groom's album:

Type of album _____

Picture size _____ quantity _____

Picture size _____ quantity _____

Picture size _____ quantity _____

Picture size _____ quantity _____

Picture size _____ quantity _____

Picture size _____ quantity _____

☐ Parents' album(s):

Type of album _____

Picture size _____ quantity _____

Picture size _____ quantity _____

☐ Extra prints:

Picture size _____ quantity _____

Picture size _____ quantity _____

Picture size _____ quantity _____

Picture size _____ quantity _____

Picture size _____ quantity _____

Picture size _____ quantity _____

Guaranteed price? ☐ yes ☐ no

Cost-of-living increase $ _____ or _____ %

Have you worked at my ceremony site? ☐ yes ☐ no

Have you worked at my reception site? ☐ yes ☐ no

If not, will you be able to visit each site before the wedding? ☐ yes ☐ no

Type of insurance carried _____

Cancellation policy _____

Subtotal   = $ _____

Sales tax   =   _____

Total   = $ _____

Deposit paid on _____ =   _____

Balance due on _____ = $ _____

Arrival time: Ceremony _____

                Reception _____

PHOTOGRAPHER

Name _____   Hours _____

Address _____   Phone _____

City _____   Fax _____

State _____ Zip _____   E-mail address _____

Contact _____   Internet _____

CONTRACTED FEE INCLUDES:

☐ Engagement pictures: number _____ Couple keeps proofs? ☐ yes ☐ no

☐ Hours at wedding _____

☐ Approximate number of pictures taken at wedding _____

☐ Proof album

☐ Negatives available until _____

☐ Bride and groom's album:

    Type of album _____

    Picture size _____ quantity _____

    Picture size _____ quantity _____

    Picture size _____ quantity _____

    Picture size _____ quantity _____

    Picture size _____ quantity _____

    Picture size _____ quantity _____

☐ Parents' album(s):

    Type of album _____

    Picture size _____ quantity _____

    Picture size _____ quantity _____

continued

☐ Extra prints:

Picture size _____ quantity _____

Picture size _____ quantity _____

Picture size _____ quantity _____

Picture size _____ quantity _____

Picture size _____ quantity _____

Picture size _____ quantity _____

Guaranteed price? ☐ yes ☐ no

Cost-of-living increase $ _____ or _____ %

Have you worked at my ceremony site? ☐ yes ☐ no

Have you worked at my reception site? ☐ yes ☐ no

If not, will you be able to visit each site before the wedding? ☐ yes ☐ no

Type of insurance carried _____

Cancellation policy _____

Subtotal   = $ _____

Sales tax   = _____

Total   = $ _____

Deposit paid on _____   = _____

Balance due on _____   = $ _____

Arrival time: Ceremony _____

                 Reception _____

PHOTOGRAPHER

Name _____   Hours _____

Address _____   Phone _____

City _____   Fax _____

State _____ Zip _____   E-mail address _____

Contact _____   Internet _____

CONTRACTED FEE INCLUDES:

☐ Engagement pictures: number _____ Couple keeps proofs? ☐ yes ☐ no

☐ Hours at wedding _____

☐ Approximate number of pictures taken at wedding _____

☐ Proof album

☐ Negatives available until _____

☐ Bride and groom's album:

Type of album _____

Picture size _____ quantity _____

Picture size _____ quantity _____

Picture size _____ quantity _____

Picture size _____ quantity _____

Picture size _____ quantity _____

Picture size _____ quantity _____

☐ Parents' album(s):

Type of album _____

Picture size _____ quantity _____

Picture size _____ quantity _____

☐ Extra prints:

Picture size _____ quantity _____

Picture size _____ quantity _____

Picture size _____ quantity _____

Picture size _____ quantity _____

Picture size _____ quantity _____

Picture size _____ quantity _____

Guaranteed price? ☐ yes ☐ no

Cost-of-living increase $ _____ or _____ %

Have you worked at my ceremony site? ☐ yes ☐ no

Have you worked at my reception site? ☐ yes ☐ no

If not, will you be able to visit each site before the wedding? ☐ yes ☐ no

Type of insurance carried _____

Cancellation policy _____

Subtotal   = $ _____

Sales tax   =   _____

Total   = $ _____

Deposit paid on _____   =   _____

Balance due on _____   = $ _____

Arrival time: Ceremony _____

Reception _____

VIDEOGRAPHER

Name _____   Hours _____

Address _____   Phone _____

City _____   Fax _____

State _____ Zip _____   E-mail address _____

Contact _____   Internet _____

BASE FEE INCLUDES: (* = extra charge)

☐ Hours at wedding _____

☐ Approximate hours of original video _____

☐ Montage of pictures at the beginning of the finished video

☐ Summary of wedding at the end of the finished video

☐ Special effects _____

☐ Requested background music _____

☐ Other editing _____

☐ Additional copies: cost @ $ _____

☐ Special (fancy) video case: cost @ $ _____

☐ Number of cameras and operators _____

☐ Number of lights and operators _____

☐ Other _____

Guaranteed price? ☐ yes ☐ no

Cost-of-living increase $ _____ or _____ %

Have you worked at my ceremony site?   ☐ yes ☐ no

Have you worked at my reception site? ☐ yes ☐ no

If not, will you be able to visit each site before the wedding?   ☐ yes ☐ no

Subtotal   = $ _____

Sales tax   =   _____

Total   = $ _____

Deposit paid on _____ =   _____

Balance due on _____ = $ _____

Arrival time: Ceremony _____

                 Reception _____

VIDEOGRAPHER

Name _____   Hours _____
Address _____   Phone _____
City _____   Fax _____
State _____ Zip _____   E-mail address _____
Contact _____   Internet _____

BASE FEE INCLUDES: (* = extra charge)

☐ Hours at wedding _____
☐ Approximate hours of original video _____
☐ Montage of pictures at the beginning of the finished video
☐ Summary of wedding at the end of the finished video
☐ Special effects _____
☐ Requested background music _____
☐ Other editing _____
☐ Additional copies: cost @ $ _____
☐ Special (fancy) video case: cost @ $ _____
☐ Number of cameras and operators _____
☐ Number of lights and operators _____
☐ Other _____

Guaranteed price? ☐ yes ☐ no
Cost-of-living increase $ _____ or _____ %
Have you worked at my ceremony site?   ☐ yes ☐ no
Have you worked at my reception site? ☐ yes ☐ no
If not, will you be able to visit each site before the wedding?   ☐ yes ☐ no

Subtotal   = $ _____
Sales tax   =   _____
Total   = $ _____
Deposit paid on _____   =   _____
Balance due on _____   = $ _____
Arrival time: Ceremony _____
               Reception _____

VIDEOGRAPHER

Name _____   Hours _____
Address _____   Phone _____
City _____   Fax _____
State _____ Zip _____   E-mail address _____
Contact _____   Internet _____

BASE FEE INCLUDES: (* = extra charge)

☐ Hours at wedding _____
☐ Approximate hours of original video _____
☐ Montage of pictures at the beginning of the finished video
☐ Summary of wedding at the end of the finished video
☐ Special effects _____
☐ Requested background music _____
☐ Other editing _____
☐ Additional copies: cost @ $ _____
☐ Special (fancy) video case: cost @ $ _____
☐ Number of cameras and operators _____
☐ Number of lights and operators _____
☐ Other _____

Guaranteed price? ☐ yes ☐ no
Cost-of-living increase $ _____ or _____ %
Have you worked at my ceremony site?   ☐ yes ☐ no
Have you worked at my reception site? ☐ yes ☐ no
If not, will you be able to visit each site before the wedding?   ☐ yes ☐ no

Subtotal   = $ _____
Sales tax   =   _____
Total   = $ _____
Deposit paid on _____   =   _____
Balance due on _____   = $ _____
Arrival time: Ceremony _____
                Reception _____

FLORIST

Name _____   Hours _____
Address _____   Phone _____
City _____   Fax _____
State _____ Zip _____   E-mail address _____
Contact _____   Internet _____

If using artificial flowers, are they silk, linen, or polyester? Silk flowers are more expensive and worth it: they are the most realistic in appearance and their color fades evenly. If you have chosen fresh flowers, are they available at in-season prices? Wedding/party favors (chocolate candy in a preprinted box) are also an option.

Item	Description	Qty.	Unit Cost	Total Cost
Bridal bouquet	_____	___	_____	_____
Maid of honor bouquet	_____	___	_____	_____
Matron of honor bouquet	_____	___	_____	_____
Bridesmaid(s) bouquet(s)	_____	___	_____	_____
Junior bridesmaid(s) bouquet(s)	_____	___	_____	_____
Flower girl(s) basket(s)	_____	___	_____	_____
Toss-away bouquet	_____	___	_____	_____
Corsage(s): mother(s)	_____	___	_____	_____
Corsage(s): grandmother(s)	_____	___	_____	_____
Boutonniere: groom	_____	___	_____	_____
Boutonniere: best man	_____	___	_____	_____
Boutonniere(s): father(s)	_____	___	_____	_____
Boutonniere(s): grandfather(s)	_____	___	_____	_____
Boutonniere(s): usher(s)	_____	___	_____	_____
Boutonniere(s): junior usher(s)	_____	___	_____	_____
Boutonniere(s): ring bearer(s)	_____	___	_____	_____
Table centerpieces (guests to take these home?)	_____	___	_____	_____
Buffet centerpiece(s)	_____	___	_____	_____
Trees for *chuppah* area	_____	___	_____	_____
Floral *chuppah*	_____	___	_____	_____
Aisle runner	_____	___	_____	_____
Bows to reserve rows	_____	___	_____	_____
Rose petals (to throw instead of rice)	_____	___	_____	_____
Bathroom displays	_____	___	_____	_____

continued

Item	Description	Qty.	Unit Cost	Total Cost
Floral arrangement/fruit basket (guests' hotel rooms)	_____	__	_____	_____
Miscellaneous flowers (cake and place card tables)	_____	__	_____	_____
Linens: tablecloths	_____	__	_____	_____
napkins	_____	__	_____	_____
Bridal bouquet preservation	_____	__	_____	_____
Wedding/party favors	_____	__	_____	_____
Other	_____	__	_____	_____

Subtotal = $ _____ *

Sales tax = _____

Total = $ _____

Deposit paid on _____ = _____

Balance due on _____ = $ _____

*Includes delivery? ☐ yes ☐ no Date _____ Place _____ Time _____

*Guaranteed price? ☐ yes ☐ no

*Cost-of-living increase $ _____ or _____ %

FLORIST

Name _____   Hours _____

Address _____   Phone _____

City _____   Fax _____

State _____ Zip _____   E-mail address _____

Contact _____   Internet _____

If using artificial flowers, are they silk, linen, or polyester? Silk flowers are more expensive and worth it: they are the most realistic in appearance and their color fades evenly. If you have chosen fresh flowers, are they available at in-season prices? Wedding/party favors (chocolate candy in a preprinted box) are also an option.

Item	Description	Qty.	Unit Cost	Total Cost
Bridal bouquet	_____	__	_____	_____
Maid of honor bouquet	_____	__	_____	_____
Matron of honor bouquet	_____	__	_____	_____
Bridesmaid(s) bouquet(s)	_____	__	_____	_____
Junior bridesmaid(s) bouquet(s)	_____	__	_____	_____
Flower girl(s) basket(s)	_____	__	_____	_____
Toss-away bouquet	_____	__	_____	_____
Corsage(s): mother(s)	_____	__	_____	_____
Corsage(s): grandmother(s)	_____	__	_____	_____

Item	Description	Qty.	Unit Cost	Total Cost
Boutonniere: groom	_____	__	_____	_____
Boutonniere: best man	_____	__	_____	_____
Boutonniere(s): father(s)	_____	__	_____	_____
Boutonniere(s): grandfather(s)	_____	__	_____	_____
Boutonniere(s): usher(s)	_____	__	_____	_____
Boutonniere(s): junior usher(s)	_____	__	_____	_____
Boutonniere(s): ring bearer(s)	_____	__	_____	_____
Table centerpieces (guests to take these home?)	_____	__	_____	_____
Buffet centerpiece(s)	_____	__	_____	_____
Trees for *chuppah* area	_____	__	_____	_____
Floral *chuppah*	_____	__	_____	_____
Aisle runner	_____	__	_____	_____
Bows to reserve rows	_____	__	_____	_____
Rose petals (to throw instead of rice)	_____	__	_____	_____
Bathroom displays	_____	__	_____	_____
Floral arrangement/fruit basket (guests' hotel rooms)	_____	__	_____	_____
Miscellaneous flowers (cake and place card tables)	_____	__	_____	_____
Linens: tablecloths	_____	__	_____	_____
napkins	_____	__	_____	_____
Bridal bouquet preservation	_____	__	_____	_____
Wedding/party favors	_____	__	_____	_____
Other	_____	__	_____	_____

Subtotal   = $ _____ *

Sales tax   = _____

Total   = $ _____

Deposit paid on _____ = _____

Balance due on _____ = $ _____

*Includes delivery? ☐ yes ☐ no Date _____ Place _____ Time _____

*Guaranteed price? ☐ yes ☐ no

*Cost-of-living increase $ _____ or _____ %

FLORIST

Name _____	Hours _____
Address _____	Phone _____
City _____	Fax _____
State _____ Zip _____	E-mail address _____
Contact _____	Internet _____

If using artificial flowers, are they silk, linen, or polyester? Silk flowers are more expensive and worth it: they are the most realistic in appearance and their color fades evenly. If you have chosen fresh flowers, are they available at in-season prices? Wedding/party favors (chocolate candy in a preprinted box) are also an option.

Item	Description	Qty.	Unit Cost	Total Cost
Bridal bouquet	_____	___	_____	_____
Maid of honor bouquet	_____	___	_____	_____
Matron of honor bouquet	_____	___	_____	_____
Bridesmaid(s) bouquet(s)	_____	___	_____	_____
Junior bridesmaid(s) bouquet(s)	_____	___	_____	_____
Flower girl(s) basket(s)	_____	___	_____	_____
Toss-away bouquet	_____	___	_____	_____
Corsage(s): mother(s)	_____	___	_____	_____
Corsage(s): grandmother(s)	_____	___	_____	_____
Boutonniere: groom	_____	___	_____	_____
Boutonniere: best man	_____	___	_____	_____
Boutonniere(s): father(s)	_____	___	_____	_____
Boutonniere(s): grandfather(s)	_____	___	_____	_____
Boutonniere(s): usher(s)	_____	___	_____	_____
Boutonniere(s): junior usher(s)	_____	___	_____	_____
Boutonniere(s): ring bearer(s)	_____	___	_____	_____
Table centerpieces (guests to take these home?)	_____	___	_____	_____
Buffet centerpiece(s)	_____	___	_____	_____
Trees for *chuppah* area	_____	___	_____	_____
Floral *chuppah*	_____	___	_____	_____
Aisle runner	_____	___	_____	_____
Bows to reserve rows	_____	___	_____	_____
Rose petals (to throw instead of rice)	_____	___	_____	_____
Bathroom displays	_____	___	_____	_____

continued

Item	Description	Qty.	Unit Cost	Total Cost
Floral arrangement/fruit basket (guests' hotel rooms)	_____	___	_____	_____
Miscellaneous flowers (cake and place card tables)	_____	___	_____	_____
Linens: tablecloths	_____	___	_____	_____
napkins	_____	___	_____	_____
Bridal bouquet preservation	_____	___	_____	_____
Wedding/party favors	_____	___	_____	_____
Other	_____	___	_____	_____

Subtotal = $ _____ *

Sales tax = _____

Total = $ _____

Deposit paid on _____ = _____

Balance due on _____ = $ _____

*Includes delivery? ☐ yes ☐ no   Date _____ Place _____ Time _____

*Guaranteed price? ☐ yes ☐ no

*Cost-of-living increase $ _____ or _____ %

KETUBBAH **WRITER OR CALLIGRAPHER**
(see Ketubbah *Information Sheet)*

Name _____   Hours _____

Address _____   Phone _____

City _____   Fax _____

State _____ Zip _____   E-mail address _____

Contact _____   Internet _____

Description of design, including any special pictures or ideas you would like incorporated into the design:

_____

_____

_____

Color scheme _____

Type of paper _____

Size _____

Mode of delivery _____   Included in cost? ☐ no ☐ yes

Order date _____   Delivery or completion date _____

Total   = $ _____

Deposit paid on _____ =   _____

Balance due on _____   = $ _____

©1985 by Seymour Hefter

©1986 by Avraham Cohen

KETUBBAH WRITER OR CALLIGRAPHER

(see Ketubbah *Information Sheet)*

Name _____   Hours _____

Address _____   Phone _____

City _____   Fax _____

State _____ Zip _____   E-mail address _____

Contact _____   Internet _____

Description of design, including any special pictures or ideas you would like incorporated into the design:

_____

_____

_____

Color scheme _____

Type of paper _____

Size _____

Mode of delivery _____   Included in cost? ☐ no ☐ yes

Order date _____   Delivery or completion date _____

Total _____ = $ _____

Deposit paid on _____ = _____

Balance due on _____ = $ _____

©1980 by **Karen Shain Schloss**

©1985 by **Patty Shaivitz Leve**

©1983 by Patty Shaivitz Leve

©1980 by Karen Shain Schloss

©1991 by Seymour Hefter

©1989 by Seymour Hefter

ENGAGEMENT PARTY

Date _____

Time _____

Address _____

City _____ State _____ Zip _____

Host _____

Place _____

Phone/Fax _____

E-mail address _____

FOOD

Caterer _____

Address _____

City _____

State _____ Zip _____

Menu _____

_____

_____

Contact _____

Hours _____

Phone/Fax _____

E-mail address _____

Total   = $ _____

Deposit paid on _____   =   _____

Balance due on _____   = $ _____

Delivery? ☐ no ☐ yes

Date _____ Time _____

Place _____

Beverages included in catering costs? ☐ no ☐ yes

Selection _____

or Liquor store _____

Address _____

City _____

State _____ Zip _____

Delivery? ☐ no ☐ yes

Total   = $ _____

Deposit paid on _____   =   _____

Balance due on _____   = $ _____

Contact _____

Phone/Fax _____

Hours _____

Date _____ Time _____

Place _____

FLOWERS

Florist _____

Address _____

City _____

State _____ Zip _____

Items _____

Total   = $ _____

Deposit paid on _____   =   _____

Balance due on _____   = $ _____

Delivery? ☐ no ☐ yes

Contact _____

Hours _____

Phone/Fax _____

E-mail address _____

Date _____ Time _____

Place _____

KIPPOT (YARMULKES)*

Name _____   Hours _____

Address _____   Phone _____

City _____   Fax _____

State _____ Zip _____   E-mail address _____

Contact _____   Internet _____

Color(s) _____

Design _____

_____

Quantity _____ Cost @ $ _____   = $ _____

Total   = $ _____

Deposit paid on _____   =   _____

Balance due on _____   = $ _____

For whom:	*Personalization*
Groom	_____
Bride's father	_____
Groom's father	_____
Bride's maternal grandfather	_____
Bride's paternal grandfather	_____
Groom's maternal grandfather	_____
Groom's paternal grandfather	_____
Best man	_____
Usher	_____
Usher	_____
Usher	_____
Usher	_____
Junior usher	_____
Junior usher	_____
Ring bearer	_____
Ring bearer	_____
Other	_____

*If you are ordering from a stationer, see Part III, expense sheet headed "Invitations, Stationery, Other Items."

BRIDE'S ATTIRE

Item	Store or Person	Cost
Wedding gown*	_____	$ _____
Veil or hat	_____	_____
Shoes	_____	_____
Undergarments:	_____	_____
Bra	_____	_____
Crinoline	_____	_____
Garter	_____	_____
Garter belt	_____	_____
Pantyhose or hose	_____	_____
Petticoat	_____	_____
Other	_____	_____
Gloves	_____	_____
Handbag	_____	_____
Jewelry	_____	_____
Something old	_____	_____
Something new	_____	_____
Something borrowed	_____	_____
Something blue	_____	_____
Preservation:		
gown	_____	_____
veil	_____	_____
accessories (gloves, ring		
pillow(s), bag with glass)	_____	_____

Total $ _____

* Consider borrowing a wedding gown and/or veil from a wedding gown
  loan service. Call your local Jewish Information Service for referrals,
  Libby in Baltimore, MD (410-578-1358) or Mrs. Cohen in Lakewood, NJ (908-370-8994).

FITTINGS AND/OR ALTERATIONS
(Don't forget to take your undergarments and your shoes!)

First Fitting (when gown arrives)

Date _____ Time _____

Second Fitting (1 to 2 weeks later, if necessary)

Date _____ Time _____

Final Fitting (week before or week of the wedding)

Date _____ Time _____

GROOM'S ATTIRE

	Cost
Jewelry (cuff links, studs, tie clasp)	$ _____
Kippah (*yarmulke*)	_____
Kittel	_____
Shirt	_____
Shoes (and socks)	_____
Suit or tuxedo and accessories	_____
Tie or bow tie	_____
Total	$ _____

FORMAL WEAR--MEN

(Take a color swatch from the bridesmaids' dresses.)

Store 1 _____   Hours _____

Address _____   Phone _____

City _____   Fax _____

State _____   Zip _____   E-mail address _____

Contact _____   Internet _____

Tuxedos:	*Price*
Two-piece, regular	$ _____
Three-piece, regular	_____
Two-piece, tails	_____
Three-piece, tails	_____
Alterations included? ☐ no ☐ yes $	_____

Accessories included:

☐ Ascot: color(s) _____

☐ Bow tie: color(s) _____

☐ Cummerbund: color(s) _____

☐ Shirt: color _____ style _____

☐ Shoes: size _____

☐ Socks: color _____

Subtotal	= $ _____	Order date _____
Sales tax	= _____	Pick up on _____
Total	= $ _____	Return on _____
Deposit paid on _____	= _____	
Balance due on _____	= $ _____	

FORMAL WEAR--MEN

(Take a color swatch from the bridesmaids' dresses.)

Store 2 _____   Hours _____

Address _____   Phone _____

City _____   Fax _____

State _____ Zip _____   E-mail address _____

Contact _____   Internet _____

Tuxedos: *Price*

Two-piece, regular $ _____

Three-piece, regular   _____

Two-piece, tails   _____

Three-piece, tails   _____

Alterations included? ☐ no ☐ yes $ _____

Accessories included:

☐ Ascot: color(s) _____

☐ Bow tie: color(s) _____

☐ Cummerbund: color(s) _____

☐ Shirt: color _____ style _____

☐ Shoes: size _____

☐ Socks: color _____

Subtotal   = $ _____   Order date _____

Sales tax   =   _____   Pick up on _____

Total   = $ _____   Return on _____

Deposit paid on _____ =   _____

Balance due on _____ = $ _____

FORMAL WEAR--MEN

(Take a color swatch from the bridesmaids' dresses.)

Store 3 _____   Hours _____

Address _____   Phone _____

City _____   Fax _____

State _____ Zip _____   E-mail address _____

Contact _____   Internet _____

Tuxedos: *Price*

Two-piece, regular $ _____

Three-piece, regular   _____

Two-piece, tails   _____

Three-piece, tails   _____

Alterations included?   ☐ no ☐ yes $ _____

Accessories included:

☐ Ascot: color(s) _____

☐ Bow tie: color(s) _____

☐ Cummerbund: color(s) _____

☐ Shirt: color _____ style _____

☐ Shoes: size _____

☐ Socks: color _____

Subtotal   = $ _____   Order date _____

Sales tax   =   _____   Pick up on _____

Total   = $ _____   Return on _____

Deposit paid on _____ =   _____

Balance due on _____ = $ _____

NOTES

HONEYMOON

TRAVEL AGENCY

Name _____ Hours _____

Address _____ Phone _____

City _____ Fax _____

State _____ Zip _____ E-mail address _____

Contact _____ Internet _____

REPRESENTATIVE AT DESTINATION

Name _____ Hours _____

Address _____ Phone _____

City _____ Fax _____

State _____ Zip _____ E-mail address _____

Contact _____ Internet _____

DETAILS

Transportation:

Cost $ _____ Confirmation date _____

Name _____ Hours _____

Address _____ Phone _____

City _____ Fax _____

State _____ Zip _____ E-mail address _____

Contact _____ Internet _____

Departure date _____ Time _____

Arrival date _____ Time _____

Name _____ Hours _____

Address _____ Phone _____

City _____ Fax _____

State _____ Zip _____ E-mail address _____

Contact _____ Internet _____

Departure date _____ Time _____

Arrival date _____ Time _____

Car Rental Agency:

Name _____ Hours _____

Address _____ Phone _____

City _____ Fax _____

State _____ Zip _____ E-mail address _____

Contact _____ Internet _____

Type of car _____ Confirmation number _____

Pickup date _____ Cost $ _____

Drop-off date _____ Deposit paid on _____

Insurance required? ☐ no ☐ yes Balance due on _____

Accommodations:

Name _____   Hours _____
Address _____   Phone _____
City _____   Fax _____
State _____ Zip _____ E-mail address _____
Contact _____   Internet _____
Confirmation date _____   Confirmation number _____

Description _____ Cost $ _____
Breakfast? ☐ no ☐ yes Check-in time _____ Check-out time _____

Meals:

Plan? ☐ no ☐ yes Includes: _____
_____

Itinerary: _____
_____
_____
_____

House, Plant, and/or Pet Sitter:

Name _____   Hours _____
Address _____   Phone _____
City _____   Fax _____
State _____ Zip _____ E-mail address _____
Contact _____   Internet _____

Don't Forget!

☐ Address book   ☐ Foreign currency
☐ Birth certificates*   ☐ International driver's license
☐ Carry-on bag**   ☐ Journal/diary
☐ Copies of itinerary   ☐ Luggage (proper size)
☐ Credit cards   ☐ Marriage license
☐ Driver's licenses   ☐ Medical insurance cards
☐ Emergency phone numbers   ☐ Passports
☐ Extra pair of glasses or contact lenses ☐ Tickets
☐ Foreign country car insurance checks   ☐ Traveler's checks

Do you want to temporarily stop delivery of your mail and newspaper? ☐ no ☐ yes

*A copy, not the original.
**Pack at least one change of clothes and other necessities (sexy sleepwear--both of you!, toiletries and birth control) in case you and your luggage arrive at different destinations.

CALLIGRAPHER--INVITATIONS AND PLACE CARDS

Name _____   Hours _____

Address _____   Phone _____

City _____   Fax _____

State _____ Zip _____   E-mail address _____

Contact _____   Internet _____

INVITATIONS

Inner envelope at $ _____ x Qty _____ = $ _____

Outer envelope at $ _____ x Qty _____ = _____

Total = $ _____

Deposit paid on _____ = _____

Balance paid on _____ = $ _____

Order date _____

PLACE CARDS

Place cards at $ _____ x Qty _____ = $ _____

Balance paid on _____ = $ _____

Order date _____   Pickup date _____

CALLIGRAPHER--INVITATIONS AND PLACE CARDS

Name _____   Hours _____

Address _____   Phone _____

City _____   Fax _____

State _____ Zip _____   E-mail address _____

Contact _____   Internet _____

INVITATIONS

Inner envelope at $ _____ x Qty _____ = $ _____

Outer envelope at $ _____ x Qty _____ = _____

Total = $ _____

Deposit paid on _____ = _____

Balance paid on _____ = $ _____

Order date _____

PLACE CARDS

Place cards at $ _____ x Qty _____ = $ _____

Balance paid on _____ = $ _____

Order date _____   Pickup date _____

TRANSPORTATION

(Try a limousine, horse and buggy or a golf cart!)

Name _____   Hours _____

Address _____   Phone _____

City _____   Fax _____

State _____ Zip _____   E-mail address _____

Type _____   Internet _____

Contact _____   Total $ _____

Cost $ _____ Hours _____   Deposit paid on _____   _____

Balance due on _____ $ _____

	Departure	*Arrival*
First place	_____	_____
Time	_____	_____
Next place	_____	_____
Time	_____	_____
Next place	_____	_____
Time	_____	_____

TRANSPORTATION

(Try a limousine, horse and buggy or a golf cart!)

Name _____   Hours _____

Address _____   Phone _____

City _____   Fax _____

State _____ Zip _____   E-mail address _____

Type _____   Internet _____

Contact _____   Total $ _____

Cost $ _____ Hours _____   Deposit paid on _____   _____

Balance due on _____ $ _____

	Departure	*Arrival*
First place	_____	_____
Time	_____	_____
Next place	_____	_____
Time	_____	_____
Next place	_____	_____
Time	_____	_____

MISCELLANEOUS EXPENSES

Name _____   Hours _____
Address _____   Phone _____
City _____   Fax _____
State _____ Zip _____   E-mail address _____
Contact _____   Internet _____

Description _____
_____
_____
_____

Subtotal   = $ _____
Sales tax   =   _____
Total   = $ _____ Includes delivery? ☐ no ☐ yes
Deposit paid on _____   =   _____ Date _____ Time _____
Balance due on _____   = $ _____ Place _____

MISCELLANEOUS EXPENSES

Name _____   Hours _____
Address _____   Phone _____
City _____   Fax _____
State _____ Zip _____   E-mail address _____
Contact _____   Internet _____

Description _____
_____
_____
_____

Subtotal   = $ _____
Sales tax   =   _____
Total   = $ _____ Includes delivery? ☐ no ☐ yes
Deposit paid on _____   =   _____ Date _____ Time _____
Balance due on _____   = $ _____ Place _____

MISCELLANEOUS EXPENSES

Name _____   Hours _____
Address _____   Phone _____
City _____   Fax _____
State _____ Zip _____   E-mail address _____
Contact _____   Internet _____

Description _____
_____
_____
_____

Subtotal   = $ _____
Sales tax   =   _____
Total   = $ _____ Includes delivery? ☐ no ☐ yes
Deposit paid on _____ =   _____ Date _____ Time _____
Balance due on _____   = $ _____ Place _____

MISCELLANEOUS EXPENSES

Name _____   Hours _____
Address _____   Phone _____
City _____   Fax _____
State _____ Zip _____   E-mail address _____
Contact _____   Internet _____

Description _____
_____
_____
_____

Subtotal   = $ _____
Sales tax   =   _____
Total   = $ _____ Includes delivery? ☐ no ☐ yes
Deposit paid on _____ =   _____ Date _____ Time _____
Balance due on _____   = $ _____ Place _____

TROUSSEAU

Each woman has individual needs and dreams for her personal trousseau. Use the space provided below to list those items that you want and need and to keep track of your purchases. Include business and casual clothes, dress and party clothes, special luxuries for the honeymoon, lingerie, gloves, handbags, hats, and other heirloom items. Remember to buy a special dress for your groom's *Aufruf*, if there will be one.

Item	Cost	Paid (How, When)
_____	$ _____	_____
_____	_____	_____
_____	_____	_____
_____	_____	_____
_____	_____	_____
_____	_____	_____
_____	_____	_____
_____	_____	_____
_____	_____	_____
_____	_____	_____
_____	_____	_____
_____	_____	_____
_____	_____	_____
_____	_____	_____
_____	_____	_____
_____	_____	_____
_____	_____	_____
_____	_____	_____
_____	_____	_____
_____	_____	_____
_____	_____	_____
_____	_____	_____
_____	_____	_____
_____	_____	_____
_____	_____	_____
_____	_____	_____
_____	_____	_____
_____	_____	_____

AUFRUF

Date _____   Time _____

Synagogue _____   Contact _____

Address _____   Phone _____

City _____   Fax _____

State _____ Zip _____   E-mail address _____

Donation paid on _____ $ _____   Internet _____

ALIYOT   *English Name*   *Hebrew Name*

Groom

_____ _____ _____

_____ _____ _____

_____ _____ _____

_____ _____ _____

_____ _____ _____

FLOWERS

Florist _____   Hours _____

Address _____   Phone _____

City _____ State _____   Fax _____

Contact _____   E-mail address _____

Description _____

Total paid on _____ $ _____   Includes delivery? ☐ no   ☐ yes

Where will the flowers go at the end of the day? _____

   (i.e., family homes, nursing home, children's ward of hospital)

Who will arrange this? _____ Phone _____

CANDY AND NUT BAGS (TO THROW)

Person in charge _____   Phone _____

Preparation: Date _____ Time _____ Place _____

Contents _____

Wrapping: baggies? _____ colored plastic wrap? _____ tulle lace? _____

Ribbons: colored? _____ personalized? _____

Quantity needed _____

KIDDUSH/LUNCH

At home? ☐ no ☐ yes   At synagogue? ☐ no ☐ yes

Caterer* _____   Hours _____

Address _____   Phone _____

City _____   Fax _____

State _____ Zip _____   E-mail address _____

Contact _____   Internet _____

Menu

Food _____

Beverages _____

Delivery date _____ Time _____

Total paid on _____ $ _____

Who is supplying?

    tablecloths _____

    paper goods _____

    tables _____

    chairs _____

    coat rack/hangers _____

    wine for *Kiddush* _____

What happens to the leftovers? _____

*Family and friends will often be very happy to cook or bake.

CHUPPAH

(See section entitled "Other Things You Should Know")

Included with ceremony site? ☐ no   ☐ yes

Designer _____   Hours _____

Address _____   Phone _____

City _____   Fax _____

State _____ Zip _____   E-mail address _____

Contact _____   Internet _____

Colors _____

Design _____

Type of fabric _____   Dimensions _____

Total   = $ _____   Order date _____

Deposit paid on _____ =   _____   Shipment date _____

Balance due on _____ = $ _____   *or* Pickup date _____

POLES

Cost $ _____   Purchased from _____

CHUPPAH

(See section entitled "Other Things You Should Know")

Included with ceremony site? ☐ no   ☐ yes

Designer _____   Hours _____

Address _____   Phone _____

City _____   Fax _____

State _____ Zip _____   E-mail address _____

Contact _____   Internet _____

Colors _____

Design _____

Type of fabric _____   Dimensions _____

Total   = $ _____   Order date _____

Deposit paid on _____ =   _____   Shipment date _____

Balance due on _____ = $ _____   *or* Pickup date _____

POLES

Cost $ _____   Purchased from _____

INVITATIONS, STATIONERY, OTHER ITEMS

Some couples prefer a custom-designed invitation which may include a favorite photograph, unique graphic or original drawing. If you have the time, explore your options. Remember to save a few of each item for keepsakes.

Name _____   Hours _____

Address _____   Phone _____

City _____   Fax _____

State _____ Zip _____   E-mail address _____

Contact _____   Internet _____

	Qty	Cost
Invitations:		
Invitations	_____	$ _____
Response cards	_____	_____
Envelopes (sets)	_____	_____
Extra envelopes (sets)	25	_____
Printed directions and/or map	_____	_____
Name-retention or hyphenation notices	_____	_____
Drop shipment of extra envelopes ☐ no ☐ yes	_____	_____
Order date _____ Pickup date _____		
Announcements and envelopes:	_____	_____
Order date _____ Pickup date _____		
Informals and envelopes (bride's name only):	_____	_____
Drop shipment of envelopes ☐ no ☐ yes		
Order date _____ Pickup date _____		
Informals and envelopes (both names):	_____	_____
Drop shipment of envelopes ☐ no ☐ yes		
Order date _____ Pickup date _____		
Benchers (*for Grace After the Meal*):	_____	_____
Order date _____ Pickup date _____		
Kippot (yarmulkes): (Includes matching bobby pins? ☐ no ☐ yes)	_____	_____
Order date _____ Pickup date _____		
Place cards:	_____	_____
Order date _____ Pickup date _____		
Cocktail napkins:	_____	_____
Order date _____ Pickup date _____		

	Qty	Cost

Match packs:

    Order date _____ Pickup date _____

Guest registry and fancy feather pen:

    Order date _____ Pickup date _____

Bridal memories book:

    Order date _____ Pickup date _____

Cake knife: (You may get this as a gift.)

    Order date _____ Pickup date _____

Toasting glasses:

    Order date _____ Pickup date _____

Embosser (return address for invitations):

    Order date _____ Pickup date _____

Favors

    Order date _____ Pickup date _____

INVITATIONS, STATIONERY, OTHER ITEMS

Some couples prefer a custom-designed invitation which may include a favorite photograph, unique graphic or original drawing. If you have the time, explore your options. Remember to save a few of each item for keepsakes.

Name _____   Hours _____

Address _____   Phone _____

City _____   Fax _____

State _____ Zip _____   E-mail address _____

Contact _____   Internet _____

	Qty	Cost
Invitations:		
Invitations	_____	$ _____
Response cards	_____	_____
Envelopes (sets)	_____	_____
Extra envelopes (sets)	25	_____
Printed directions and/or map	_____	_____
Name-retention or hyphenation notices	_____	_____
Drop shipment of extra envelopes ☐ no ☐ yes	_____	_____

     Order date _____ Pickup date _____

Announcements and envelopes:	_____	_____

     Order date _____ Pickup date _____

***Informals and envelopes** (bride's name only):*	_____	_____

Drop shipment of envelopes ☐ no ☐ yes

     Order date _____ Pickup date _____

***Informals and envelopes** (both names):*	_____	_____

Drop shipment of envelopes ☐ no ☐ yes

     Order date _____ Pickup date _____

Benchers *(for Grace After the Meal):*	_____	_____

     Order date _____ Pickup date _____

Kippot (yarmulkes): (Includes matching bobby pins? ☐ no ☐ yes*)*	_____	_____

     Order date _____ Pickup date _____

Place cards:	_____	_____

     Order date _____ Pickup date _____

Cocktail napkins:	_____	_____

     Order date _____ Pickup date _____

	Qty	Cost

Match packs: _____ _____

    Order date _____ Pickup date _____

Guest registry and fancy feather pen: _____ _____

    Order date _____ Pickup date _____

Bridal memories book: _____ _____

    Order date _____ Pickup date _____

Cake knife: (You may get this as a gift.) _____ _____

    Order date _____ Pickup date _____

Toasting glasses: _____ _____

    Order date _____ Pickup date _____

Embosser (return address for invitations): _____ _____

    Order date _____ Pickup date _____

Favors

    Order date _____ Pickup date _____

INVITATIONS, STATIONERY, OTHER ITEMS

Some couples prefer a custom-designed invitation which may include a favorite photograph, unique graphic or original drawing. If you have the time, explore your options. Remember to save a few of each item for keepsakes.

Name _____   Hours _____

Address _____   Phone _____

City _____   Fax _____

State _____ Zip _____   E-mail address _____

Contact _____   Internet _____

	Qty	Cost
Invitations:		
Invitations	_____	$ _____
Response cards	_____	_____
Envelopes (sets)	_____	_____
Extra envelopes (sets)	25	_____
Printed directions and/or map	_____	_____
Name-retention or hyphenation notices	_____	_____
Drop shipment of extra envelopes ☐ no ☐ yes	_____	_____

Order date _____ Pickup date _____

Announcements and envelopes:	_____	_____

Order date _____ Pickup date _____

Informals and envelopes *(bride's name only):*	_____	_____

Drop shipment of envelopes   ☐ no ☐ yes

Order date _____ Pickup date _____

Informals and envelopes *(both names):*	_____	_____

Drop shipment of envelopes   ☐ no ☐ yes

Order date _____ Pickup date _____

Benchers *(for Grace After the Meal):*	_____	_____

Order date _____ Pickup date _____

Kippot (yarmulkes): (Includes matching bobby pins? ☐ no ☐ yes*)*	_____	_____

Order date _____ Pickup date _____

Place cards:	_____	_____

Order date _____ Pickup date _____

Cocktail napkins:	_____	_____

Order date _____ Pickup date _____

	Qty	Cost

Match packs:

    Order date _____ Pickup date _____

Guest registry and fancy feather pen:

    Order date _____ Pickup date _____

Bridal memories book:

    Order date _____ Pickup date _____

Cake knife: (You may get this as a gift.)

    Order date _____ Pickup date _____

Toasting glasses:

    Order date _____ Pickup date _____

Embosser (return address for invitations):

    Order date _____ Pickup date _____

Favors

    Order date _____ Pickup date _____

Accommodations and Transportation for Out-of-Town Guests

Guest(s) _____   Phone _____

Arrival: Date _____   Time _____   Place _____

Departure: Date _____   Time _____   Place _____

Accommodations

Place _____   Hours _____

Address _____   Phone _____

City _____   Fax _____

State _____ Zip _____   E-mail address _____

Contact _____   Internet _____

From (date) _____ To _____   Cost $ _____ Paid on _____

Description _____
_____

Confirmation number _____

Transportation   *Who/What*

Arrival place to accommodations   _____

Accommodations to ceremony   _____

Ceremony to reception   _____

Reception to accommodations   _____

Accommodations to departure place   _____

Other   _____

ACCOMMODATIONS AND TRANSPORTATION FOR OUT-OF-TOWN GUESTS

Guest(s) _____   Phone _____

Arrival: Date _____ Time _____   Place _____

Departure: Date _____ Time _____   Place _____

ACCOMMODATIONS

Place _____   Hours _____

Address _____   Phone _____

City _____   Fax _____

State _____ Zip _____   E-mail address _____

Contact _____   Internet _____

From (date) _____ To _____   Cost $ _____ Paid on _____

Description _____
_____

Confirmation number _____

TRANSPORTATION   *Who/What*

Arrival place to accommodations   _____

Accommodations to ceremony   _____

Ceremony to reception   _____

Reception to accommodations   _____

Accommodations to departure place   _____

Other   _____

ACCOMMODATIONS AND TRANSPORTATION FOR OUT-OF-TOWN GUESTS

Guest(s) _____ Phone _____

Arrival: Date _____ Time _____   Place _____

Departure: Date _____ Time _____   Place _____

ACCOMMODATIONS

Place _____   Hours _____

Address _____   Phone _____

City _____   Fax _____

State _____ Zip _____   E-mail address _____

Contact _____   Internet _____

From (date) _____ To _____   Cost $ _____ Paid on _____

Description _____

_____

Confirmation number _____

TRANSPORTATION   *Who/What*

Arrival place to accommodations   _____

Accommodations to ceremony   _____

Ceremony to reception   _____

Reception to accommodations   _____

Accommodations to departure place   _____

Other   _____

ACCOMMODATIONS AND TRANSPORTATION FOR OUT-OF-TOWN GUESTS

Guest(s) _____   Phone _____

Arrival: Date _____ Time _____   Place _____

Departure: Date _____ Time _____   Place _____

ACCOMMODATIONS

Place _____   Hours _____

Address _____   Phone _____

City _____   Fax _____

State _____ Zip _____   E-mail address _____

Contact _____   Internet _____

From (date) _____ To _____   Cost $ _____ Paid on _____

Description _____
_____

Confirmation number _____

TRANSPORTATION   *Who/What*

Arrival place to accommodations   _____

Accommodations to ceremony   _____

Ceremony to reception   _____

Reception to accommodations   _____

Accommodations to departure place   _____

Other   _____

ACCOMMODATIONS AND TRANSPORTATION FOR OUT-OF-TOWN GUESTS

Guest(s) _____   Phone _____

Arrival: Date _____ Time _____   Place _____

Departure: Date _____ Time _____   Place _____

ACCOMMODATIONS

Place _____   Hours _____

Address _____   Phone _____

City _____   Fax _____

State _____ Zip _____   E-mail address _____

Contact _____   Internet _____

From (date) _____ To _____   Cost $ _____ Paid on _____

Description _____

_____

Confirmation number _____

TRANSPORTATION   *Who/What*

Arrival place to accommodations   _____

Accommodations to ceremony   _____

Ceremony to reception   _____

Reception to accommodations   _____

Accommodations to departure place   _____

Other   _____

ACCOMMODATIONS AND TRANSPORTATION FOR OUT-OF-TOWN GUESTS

Guest(s) _____ Phone _____

Arrival: Date _____ Time _____   Place _____

Departure: Date _____ Time _____   Place _____

ACCOMMODATIONS

Place _____   Hours _____

Address _____   Phone _____

City _____   Fax _____

State _____ Zip _____   E-mail address _____

Contact _____   Internet _____

From (date) _____ To _____   Cost $ _____ Paid on _____

Description _____

_____

Confirmation number _____

TRANSPORTATION   *Who/What*

Arrival place to accommodations   _____

Accommodations to ceremony   _____

Ceremony to reception   _____

Reception to accommodations   _____

Accommodations to departure place _____

Other   _____

ACCOMMODATIONS AND TRANSPORTATION FOR OUT-OF-TOWN GUESTS

Guest(s) _____   Phone _____

Arrival: Date _____ Time _____   Place _____

Departure: Date _____ Time _____   Place _____

ACCOMMODATIONS

Place _____   Hours _____

Address _____   Phone _____

City _____   Fax _____

State _____ Zip _____   E-mail address _____

Contact _____   Internet _____

From (date) _____ To _____   Cost $ _____ Paid on _____

Description _____
_____

Confirmation number _____

TRANSPORTATION   *Who/What*

Arrival place to accommodations   _____

Accommodations to ceremony   _____

Ceremony to reception   _____

Reception to accommodations   _____

Accommodations to departure place   _____

Other   _____

ACCOMMODATIONS AND TRANSPORTATION FOR OUT-OF-TOWN GUESTS

Guest(s) _____   Phone _____

Arrival: Date _____ Time _____   Place _____

Departure: Date _____ Time _____   Place _____

ACCOMMODATIONS

Place _____   Hours _____

Address _____   Phone _____

City _____   Fax _____

State _____ Zip _____   E-mail address _____

Contact _____   Internet _____

From (date) _____ To _____   Cost $ _____ Paid on _____

Description _____
_____

Confirmation number _____

TRANSPORTATION   *Who/What*

Arrival place to accommodations   _____

Accommodations to ceremony   _____

Ceremony to reception   _____

Reception to accommodations   _____

Accommodations to departure place   _____

Other   _____

LIQUOR, WINE, AND CHAMPAGNE

Try to find a store that will deliver your order to the reception site *and* pick up unopened bottles. Many liquor stores will sell to you on a consignment basis: pay for only what you use. Also, remember that name brands are more expensive and often not necessary. Ask your caterer or liquor merchant to help you order quantities and brands most suited for the guests at your *simcha*. Here is a guide for a crowd of 150 average Jewish drinkers. Fill in your quantities in the next chart.

Item	*Quantity*
Beer (Domestic, Foreign, Micro-brews	2-4 cases
Bottled water	1-2 cases
Bourbon	1 bottle
Champagne	2 cases
Gin	1 bottle
Punch (as main beverage)	8 gallons
Rum	2 bottles
Scotch	2 bottles
Sparkling cider	4 bottles
Soda, mixers, mineral water, tonic	(ask your supplier)
Various liqueurs (Kahlua, Amaretto, chocolate mint, etc.)	1 bottle each
Vodka	1 bottle
Whiskey	1 bottle
Wine	6 cases
Wine Coolers	4 cases

Store 1 _____   Hours _____

Address _____   Phone _____

City _____   Fax _____

State _____ Zip _____   E-mail address _____

Contact _____   Internet _____

Item/Brand	*Size*	*Quantity*	*Each*	*Total*
_____	_____	_____	$ _____	$ _____
_____	_____	_____	_____	_____
_____	_____	_____	_____	_____
_____	_____	_____	_____	_____
_____	_____	_____	_____	_____
_____	_____	_____	_____	_____
_____	_____	_____	_____	_____
_____	_____	_____	_____	_____
_____	_____	_____	_____	_____
_____	_____	_____	_____	_____
_____	_____	_____	_____	_____

Order date _____   Subtotal   = $ _____

Delivery: Date _____   Sales tax _____ %   =   _____

          Time _____   Total   = $ _____

          Place _____   Deposit paid on _____   =

Pickup: Date _____   Balance due on _____   = $ _____

          Time _____   Less refund on _____   =   _____

          Place _____   Total expenditure _____   = $ _____

Store 2 _____   Hours _____

Address _____   Phone _____

City _____   Fax _____

State _____ Zip _____   E-mail address _____

Contact _____   Internet _____

Item/Brand	*Size*	*Quantity*	Each	*Total*
_____	_____	_____	$ _____	$ _____
_____	_____	_____	_____	_____
_____	_____	_____	_____	_____
_____	_____	_____	_____	_____
_____	_____	_____	_____	_____
_____	_____	_____	_____	_____
_____	_____	_____	_____	_____
_____	_____	_____	_____	_____
_____	_____	_____	_____	_____
_____	_____	_____	_____	_____

Order date _____   Subtotal   = $ _____

Delivery: Date _____   Sales tax _____ %   = $ _____

          Time _____   Total   = $ _____

          Place _____   Deposit paid on _____   =

Pickup: Date _____   Balance due on _____   = $ _____

          Time _____   Less refund on _____   =   _____

          Place _____   Total expenditure _____   = $ _____

Store 3 _____   Hours _____
Address _____   Phone _____
City _____   Fax _____
State _____ Zip _____   E-mail address _____
Contact _____   Internet _____

Item/Brand	*Size*	*Quantity*	*Each*	*Total*
_____	_____	_____	$ _____	$ _____
_____	_____	_____	_____	_____
_____	_____	_____	_____	_____
_____	_____	_____	_____	_____
_____	_____	_____	_____	_____
_____	_____	_____	_____	_____
_____	_____	_____	_____	_____
_____	_____	_____	_____	_____
_____	_____	_____	_____	_____
_____	_____	_____	_____	_____

Order date   _____   Subtotal   = $ _____
Delivery: Date _____   Sales tax _____ %   = _____
          Time _____   Total   = $ _____
          Place _____   Deposit paid on _____   =
Pickup: Date _____   Balance due on _____   = $ _____
          Time _____   Less refund on _____   =
          Place _____   Total expenditure _____   = $ _____

NOTES

REHEARSAL PARTY OR DINNER

Date _____   Contact _____
Time _____   Hours _____
Host _____   Phone _____
Address _____   Fax _____
City _____   E-mail address _____
State _____ Zip _____   Internet _____

FOOD

Caterer/Restaurant _____   Hours _____
Address _____   Phone _____
City _____   Fax _____
State _____ Zip _____   E-mail address _____
Contact _____   Internet _____
Menu _____
_____
_____

Cost   = $ _____

Deposit paid on _____   =   _____

Balance due on _____   = $ _____

Delivery? ☐ no   ☐ yes   Date _____ Time _____

                                     Place _____

Beverages included in catering costs? ☐ no   ☐ yes

Selection _____

or Liquor store _____   Hours _____
Address _____   Phone _____
City _____   Fax _____
State _____ Zip _____   E-mail address _____
Contact _____   Internet _____
Date _____ Time _____   Place _____
Delivery? ☐ no   ☐ yes

Cost   = $ _____

Deposit paid on _____   =   _____

Balance due on _____   = $ _____

Delivery? ☐ no   ☐ yes

FLOWERS

Florist _____   Hours _____

Address _____   Phone _____

City _____   Fax _____

State _____ Zip _____   E-mail address _____

Contact _____   Internet _____

Items _____

_____

_____

Cost   = $ _____

Deposit paid on _____   = _____

Balance due on _____   = $ _____

Delivery? ☐ no   ☐ yes   Date _____ Time _____

Place _____

BRIDE'S PERSONAL CARE

Haircut:

Stylist _____ Phone _____

Address _____ Fax _____

City _____ State _____ Zip _____ E-mail address _____

Appointment: Date _____ Internet _____

Wedding day: Place _____ Time _____ Cost $ _____

Time _____ Cost $ _____

Facial:

Beautician _____ Fax _____

Address _____ E-mail address _____

City _____ State _____ Zip _____ Internet _____

Appointment: Date _____ Time _____ Cost $ _____

Phone _____ Time _____ Cost $ _____

Manicure and Pedicure:

Beautician _____ Phone _____

Address _____ Fax _____

City _____ State _____ Zip _____ E-mail address _____

Appointment: Date _____ Internet _____

Date _____ Time _____ Manicure $ _____

Time _____ Pedicure $ _____

Waxing:

Beautician _____ Fax _____

Address _____ E-mail address _____

City _____ State _____ Zip _____ Internet _____

Appointment: Date _____ Time _____ Cost $ _____

Phone _____ Time _____ Cost $ _____

Makeup:

Makeup artist _____ Fax _____

Address _____ E-mail address _____

City _____ State _____ Zip _____ Internet _____

Appointment: Date _____ Time _____ Cost $ _____

Phone _____ Time _____ Cost $ _____

Other Appointments:

Name _____   Phone _____

Address _____   Fax _____

City _____ State _____ Zip _____   E-mail address _____

Appointment: Date _____   Internet _____

Wedding day: Place _____   Time _____ Cost $ _____

Time _____ Cost $ _____

Name _____   Phone _____

Address _____   Fax _____

City _____ State _____ Zip _____   E-mail address _____

Appointment: Date _____   Internet _____

Wedding day: Place _____   Time _____ Cost $ _____

Time _____ Cost $ _____

Additional Notes:

Sheva Berachot Celebration

Date _____   Contact _____

Time _____   Hours _____

Host _____   Phone _____

Address _____   Fax _____

City _____   E-mail address _____

State _____ Zip _____   Internet _____

Food

Caterer/Restaurant _____   Hours _____

Address _____   Phone _____

City _____   Fax _____

State _____ Zip _____   E-mail address _____

Contact _____   Internet _____

Menu _____

_____

_____

Cost   = $ _____

Deposit paid on _____ =   _____

Balance due on _____ = $ _____

Delivery? ☐ no   ☐ yes   Date _____ Time _____

                                      Place _____

Beverages included in catering costs? ☐ no   ☐ yes

Selection _____

or Liquor store _____   Hours _____

Address _____   Phone _____

City _____   Fax _____

State _____ Zip _____   E-mail address _____

Contact _____   Internet _____

Date _____ Time _____   Place _____

Delivery? ☐ no   ☐ yes

Cost   = $ _____

Deposit paid on _____ =   _____

Balance due on _____ = $ _____

*Family and friends will often be very happy to cook and bake; there also may be leftovers from the wedding meal.

Sheva Berachot Celebration

FLOWERS

Florist _____   Hours _____

Address _____   Phone _____

City _____   Fax _____

State _____ Zip _____   E-mail address _____

Contact _____   Internet _____

Items _____

_____

_____

_____

Cost   = $ _____

Deposit paid on _____ =   _____

Balance due on _____   = $ _____

Delivery? ☐ no   ☐ yes   Date _____ Time _____

                                 Place _____

SHEVA BERACHOT CELEBRATION

Date _____   Contact _____

Time _____   Hours _____

Host _____   Phone _____

Address _____   Fax _____

City _____   E-mail address _____

State _____ Zip _____   Internet _____

FOOD

Caterer/Restaurant _____   Hours _____

Address _____   Phone _____

City _____   Fax _____

State _____ Zip _____   E-mail address _____

Contact _____   Internet _____

Menu _____

_____

_____

continued

Cost   = $ _____

Deposit paid on _____ =   _____

Balance due on _____ = $ _____

Delivery? ☐ no   ☐ yes   Date _____ Time _____

               Place _____

Beverages included in catering costs? ☐ no   ☐ yes

Selection _____

or Liquor store _____ Hours _____

Address _____ Phone _____

City _____ Fax _____

State _____ Zip _____ E-mail address _____

Contact _____ Internet _____

Date _____ Time _____ Place _____

Delivery? ☐ no   ☐ yes

Cost   = $ _____

Deposit paid on _____ =   _____

Balance due on _____ = $ _____

*Family and friends will often be very happy to cook and bake; there also may be leftovers from the wedding meal.

FLOWERS

Florist _____ Hours _____

Address _____ Phone _____

City _____ Fax _____

State _____ Zip _____ E-mail address _____

Contact _____ Internet _____

Items _____

_____

_____

Cost   = $ _____

Deposit paid on _____ =   _____

Balance due on _____ = $ _____

Delivery? ☐ no   ☐ yes   Date _____ Time _____

               Place _____

CLEANING AND PRESERVING GOWN, VEIL, AND ACCESSORIES

Name _____   Hours _____

Address _____   Phone _____

City _____   Fax _____

State _____ Zip _____   E-mail address _____

Contact _____   Internet _____

Wedding gown $ _____   Includes box? or $ _____

Veil or hat $ _____

Petticoat or crinoline $ _____

Accessories $ _____   (gloves, ring pillow(s), bag with glass)

Total $ _____

Dropped off on _____   Pick up on _____

CLEANING AND PRESERVING GOWN, VEIL, AND ACCESSORIES

Name _____   Hours _____

Address _____   Phone _____

City _____   Fax _____

State _____ Zip _____   E-mail address _____

Contact _____   Internet _____

Wedding gown $ _____   Includes box? or $ _____

Veil or hat $ _____

Petticoat or crinoline $ _____

Accessories $ _____   (gloves, ring pillow(s), bag with glass)

Total $ _____

Dropped off on _____   Pick up on _____

CLEANING AND PRESERVING GOWN, VEIL, AND ACCESSORIES

Name _____   Hours _____

Address _____   Phone _____

City _____   Fax _____

State _____ Zip _____   E-mail address _____

Contact _____   Internet _____

Wedding gown $ _____   Includes box? or $ _____

Veil or hat $ _____

Petticoat or crinoline $ _____

Accessories $ _____   (gloves, ring pillow(s), bag with glass)

Total $ _____

Dropped off on _____   Pick up on _____

CLEANING AND PRESERVING GOWN, VEIL, AND ACCESSORIES

Name _____   Hours _____

Address _____   Phone _____

City _____   Fax _____

State _____ Zip _____   E-mail address _____

Contact _____   Internet _____

Wedding gown $ _____   Includes box? or $ _____

Veil or hat $ _____

Petticoat or crinoline $ _____

Accessories $ _____   (gloves, ring pillow(s), bag with glass)

Total $ _____

Dropped off on _____   Pick up on _____

NOTES

NOTES

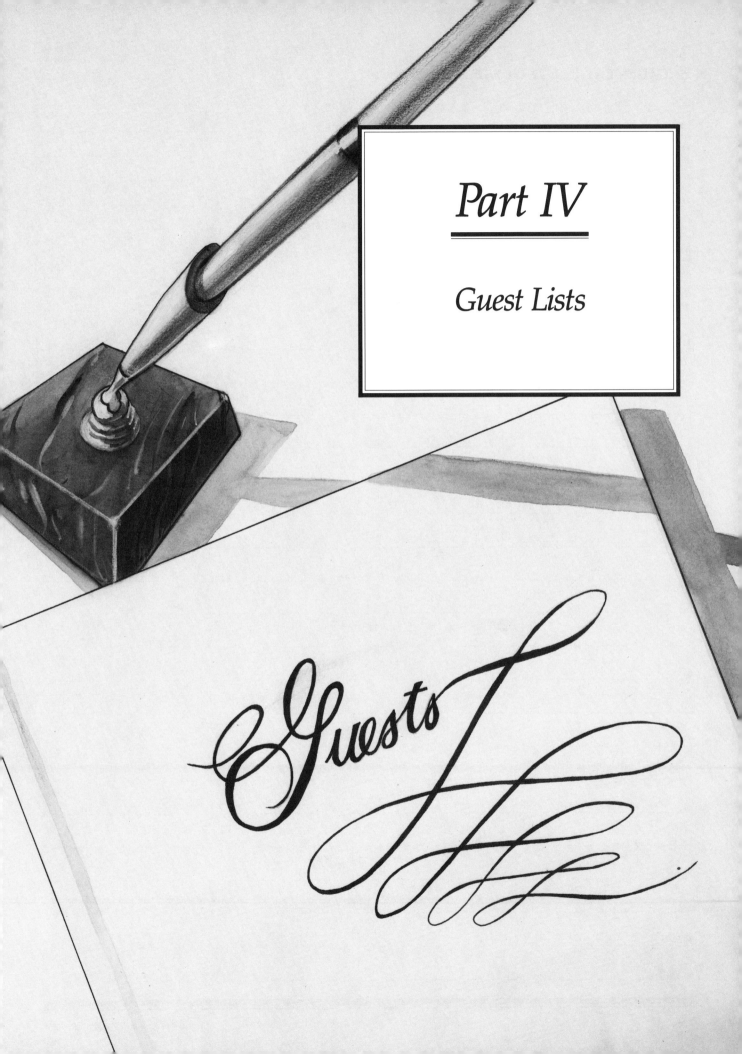

Part IV

Guest Lists

ENGAGEMENT PARTY GUEST LIST

Date _____   Time _____

Host(s) _____   Phone _____

_____   Fax _____

Address _____   E-mail address _____

City _____   Internet _____

State _____ Zip _____

NAME & ADDRESS	PHONE	NUMBER INVITED	NUMBER COMING
1. _____	_____	_____	_____
_____			
2. _____	_____	_____	_____
_____			
3. _____	_____	_____	_____
_____			
4. _____	_____	_____	_____
_____			
5. _____	_____	_____	_____
_____			
6. _____	_____	_____	_____
_____			
7. _____	_____	_____	_____
_____			
8. _____	_____	_____	_____
_____			
9. _____	_____	_____	_____
_____			
10. _____	_____	_____	_____
_____			

NAME & ADDRESS	PHONE	NUMBER INVITED	NUMBER COMING
11.			
12.			
13.			
14.			
15.			
16.			
17.			
18.			
19.			
20.			
21.			
22.			
23.			

NAME & ADDRESS	PHONE	NUMBER INVITED	NUMBER COMING
24.			
25.			
26.			
27.			
28.			
29.			
30.			
31.			
32.			
33.			
34.			
35.			
36.			

The Complete Jewish Wedding Planner

NAME & ADDRESS	PHONE	NUMBER INVITED	NUMBER COMING
37.			
38.			
39.			
40.			
41.			
42.			
43.			
44.			
45.			
46.			
47.			
48.			
49.			

NAME & ADDRESS	PHONE	NUMBER INVITED	NUMBER COMING
50.			
51.			
52.			
53.			
54.			
55.			
56.			
57.			
58.			
59.			
60.			
61.			
62.			

NAME & ADDRESS	PHONE	NUMBER INVITED	NUMBER COMING
63.			
64.			
65.			
66.			
67.			
68.			
69.			
70.			
71.			
72.			
73.			
74.			
75.			

Bride's Attendants

Maid of Honor

Name ———————————————————

Address ———————————————————

City ———————————————————

State/Zip ———————————————————

Phone/Fax ———————————————————

Car/Cellular phone/Pager ——————————

E-mail address ——————————————

Responsibilities ——————————————

———————————————————

Matron of Honor

Name ———————————————————

Address ———————————————————

City ———————————————————

State/Zip ———————————————————

Phone/Fax ———————————————————

Car/Cellular phone/Pager ——————————

E-mail address ——————————————

Responsibilities ——————————————

———————————————————

Bridesmaid

Name ———————————————————

Address ———————————————————

City ———————————————————

State/Zip ———————————————————

Phone/Fax ———————————————————

Car/Cellular phone/Pager ——————————

E-mail address ——————————————

Responsibilities ——————————————

———————————————————

Bridesmaid

Name ———————————————————

Address ———————————————————

City ———————————————————

State/Zip ———————————————————

Phone/Fax ———————————————————

Car/Cellular phone/Pager ——————————

E-mail address ——————————————

Responsibilities ——————————————

———————————————————

Bridesmaid

Name ———————————————————

Address ———————————————————

City ———————————————————

State/Zip ———————————————————

Phone/Fax ———————————————————

Car/Cellular phone/Pager ——————————

E-mail address ——————————————

Responsibilities ——————————————

———————————————————

Bridesmaid

Name ———————————————————

Address ———————————————————

City ———————————————————

State/Zip ———————————————————

Phone/Fax ———————————————————

Car/Cellular phone/Pager ——————————

E-mail address ——————————————

Responsibilities ——————————————

———————————————————

JUNIOR BRIDESMAID

Name _____

Address _____

City _____

State/Zip _____

Phone/Fax _____

Car/Cellular phone/Pager _____

E-mail address _____

Responsibilities _____

_____

JUNIOR BRIDESMAID

Name _____

Address _____

City _____

State/Zip _____

Phone/Fax _____

Car/Cellular phone/Pager _____

E-mail address _____

Responsibilities _____

_____

FLOWER GIRL

Name _____

Address _____

City _____

State/Zip _____

Phone/Fax _____

E-mail address _____

Responsibilities _____

_____

FLOWER GIRL

Name _____

Address _____

City _____

State/Zip _____

Phone/Fax _____

E-mail address _____

Responsibilities _____

_____

Groom's Attendants

Best Man

Name _____

Address _____

City _____

State/Zip _____

Phone/Fax _____

Car/Cellular phone/Pager _____

E-mail address _____

Responsibilities _____

_____

Head Usher

Name _____

Address _____

City _____

State/Zip _____

Phone/Fax _____

Car/Cellular phone/Pager _____

E-mail address _____

Responsibilities _____

_____

Usher

Name _____

Address _____

City _____

State/Zip _____

Phone/Fax _____

Car/Cellular phone/Pager _____

E-mail address _____

Responsibilities _____

_____

Usher

Name _____

Address _____

City _____

State/Zip _____

Phone/Fax _____

Car/Cellular phone/Pager _____

E-mail address _____

Responsibilities _____

_____

Usher

Name _____

Address _____

City _____

State/Zip _____

Phone/Fax _____

Car/Cellular phone/Pager _____

E-mail address _____

Responsibilities _____

_____

Usher

Name _____

Address _____

City _____

State/Zip _____

Phone/Fax _____

Car/Cellular phone/Pager _____

E-mail address _____

Responsibilities _____

_____

JUNIOR USHER

Name _____

Address _____

City _____

State/Zip _____

Phone/Fax _____

Car/Cellular phone/Pager _____

E-mail address _____

Responsibilities _____

_____

JUNIOR USHER

Name _____

Address _____

City _____

State/Zip _____

Phone/Fax _____

Car/Cellular phone/Pager _____

E-mail address _____

Responsibilities _____

_____

RING BEARER

Name _____

Address _____

City _____

State/Zip _____

Phone/Fax _____

E-mail address _____

Responsibilities _____

_____

RING BEARER

Name _____

Address _____

City _____

State/Zip _____

Phone/Fax _____

E-mail address _____

Responsibilities _____

_____

WEDDING GUEST LIST

How to limit the number of guests: Ask yourself these questions or use the formulas given.

1. Do the bride and groom know them?
2. Has it been *years* since you last saw them?
3. Are they parents' business associates?
4. Are you sure you want to invite children?

5. Invite only in-town cousins?
6. Invite only one cousin from each family?
7. Divide the list into thirds:
   ⅓ bride's family, ⅓ groom's family,
   ⅓ bride and groom's friends.

NAME & ADDRESS	PHONE	NUMBER INVITED	NUMBER COMING
1.			
2.			
3.			
4.			
5.			
6.			
7.			
8.			
9.			
10.			

NAME & ADDRESS	PHONE	NUMBER INVITED	NUMBER COMING
11.			
12.			
13.			
14.			
15.			
16.			
17.			
18.			
19.			
20.			
21.			
22.			
23.			

NAME & ADDRESS	PHONE	NUMBER INVITED	NUMBER COMING
24.			
25.			
26.			
27.			
28.			
29.			
30.			
31.			
32.			
33.			
34.			
35.			
36.			

NAME & ADDRESS	PHONE	NUMBER INVITED	NUMBER COMING
37.			
38.			
39.			
40.			
41.			
42.			
43.			
44.			
45.			
46.			
47.			
48.			
49.			

NAME & ADDRESS	PHONE	NUMBER INVITED	NUMBER COMING
50.			
51.			
52.			
53.			
54.			
55.			
56.			
57.			
58.			
59.			
60.			
61.			
62.			

NAME & ADDRESS	PHONE	NUMBER INVITED	NUMBER COMING
63.			
64.			
65.			
66.			
67.			
68.			
69.			
70.			
71.			
72.			
73.			
74.			
75.			

NAME & ADDRESS	PHONE	NUMBER INVITED	NUMBER COMING
76.			
77.			
78.			
79.			
80.			
81.			
82.			
83.			
84.			
85.			
86.			
87.			
88.			

NAME & ADDRESS	PHONE	NUMBER INVITED	NUMBER COMING
89.			
90.			
91.			
92.			
93.			
94.			
95.			
96.			
97.			
98.			
99.			
100.			
101.			

NAME & ADDRESS	PHONE	NUMBER INVITED	NUMBER COMING
102.			
103.			
104.			
105.			
106.			
107.			
108.			
109.			
110.			
111.			
112.			
113.			
114.			

NAME & ADDRESS	PHONE	NUMBER INVITED	NUMBER COMING
115.			
116.			
117.			
118.			
119.			
120.			
121.			
122.			
123.			
124.			
125.			
126.			
127.			

NAME & ADDRESS	PHONE	NUMBER INVITED	NUMBER COMING
128.			
129.			
130.			
131.			
132.			
133.			
134.			
135.			
136.			
137.			
138.			
139.			
140.			

The Complete Jewish Wedding Planner

NAME & ADDRESS	PHONE	NUMBER INVITED	NUMBER COMING
141.			
142.			
143.			
144.			
145.			
146.			
147.			
148.			
149.			
150.			

BRIDAL SHOWER GUEST LIST

Date _____   Time _____

Place _____   Phone _____

Address _____   Fax _____

City _____ State _____ Zip _____   E-mail address _____

Hostess(es) _____   Phone/Fax _____

Address _____   Car/Cellular phone/Pager _____

City _____ State _____ Zip _____   E-mail address _____

Theme _____

NAME & ADDRESS	PHONE	NUMBER INVITED	NUMBER COMING
1.			
2.			
3.			
4.			
5.			
6.			
7.			
8.			
9.			

NAME & ADDRESS	PHONE	NUMBER INVITED	NUMBER COMING
10.			
11.			
12.			
13.			
14.			
15.			
16.			
17.			
18.			
19.			
20.			
21.			
22.			

NAME & ADDRESS	PHONE	NUMBER INVITED	NUMBER COMING
23.			
24.			
25.			
26.			
27.			
28.			
29.			
30.			
31.			
32.			
33.			
34.			
35.			

NAME & ADDRESS	PHONE	NUMBER INVITED	NUMBER COMING
36.			
37.			
38.			
39.			
40.			
41.			
42.			
43.			
44.			
45.			
46.			
47.			
48.			

NAME & ADDRESS	PHONE	NUMBER INVITED	NUMBER COMING
49.			
50.			
51.			
52.			
53.			
54.			
55.			
56.			
57.			
58.			
59.			
60.			

The Complete Jewish Wedding Planner

REHEARSAL PARTY OR DINNER GUEST LIST

Date _____   Time _____

Place _____   Phone _____

Address _____   Fax _____

City _____ State _____ Zip _____   E-mail address _____

Hostess(es) _____   Phone/Fax _____

Address _____   Car/Cellular phone/Pager _____

City _____ State _____ Zip _____   E-mail address _____

Include: Bride, groom, attendants and spouses, parents, grandparents, officiants and spouses, any out-of-town guests who are already in town [Optional: musicians, photographer(s), videographer(s), party planner]

NAME & ADDRESS	PHONE	NUMBER INVITED	NUMBER COMING
1.			
2.			
3.			
4.			
5.			
6.			
7.			
8.			

NAME & ADDRESS	PHONE	NUMBER INVITED	NUMBER COMING
9.			
10.			
11.			
12.			
13.			
14.			
15.			
16.			
17.			
18.			
19.			
20.			
21.			

NAME & ADDRESS	PHONE	NUMBER INVITED	NUMBER COMING
22.			
23.			
24.			
25.			
26.			
27.			
28.			
29.			
30.			
31.			
32.			
33.			
34.			

35. _____ _____ _____ _____

_____

36. _____ _____ _____ _____

_____

37. _____ _____ _____ _____

_____

38. _____ _____ _____ _____

_____

39. _____ _____ _____ _____

_____

40. _____ _____ _____ _____

_____

41. _____ _____ _____ _____

_____

42. _____ _____ _____ _____

_____

43. _____ _____ _____ _____

_____

44. _____ _____ _____ _____

_____

45. _____ _____ _____ _____

_____

46. _____ _____ _____ _____

_____

47. _____ _____ _____ _____

_____

NAME & ADDRESS	PHONE	NUMBER INVITED	NUMBER COMING
48.			
49.			
50.			
51.			
52.			
53.			
54.			
55.			
56.			
57.			
58.			
59.			
60.			

Bridal Party Luncheon Guest List

Date _____ Time _____

Place _____ Phone/Fax _____

Address _____ Car/Cellular phone/Pager _____

City _____ State _____ Zip _____ E-mail address _____

Hostess (bride) _____

NAME & ADDRESS	PHONE	NUMBER INVITED	NUMBER COMING
1.			
2.			
3.			
4.			
5.			
6.			
7.			
8.			
9.			
10.			

NAME & ADDRESS	PHONE	NUMBER INVITED	NUMBER COMING
11.			
12.			
13.			
14.			
15.			
16.			
17.			
18.			
19.			
20.			
21.			
22.			
23.			

NAME & ADDRESS	PHONE	NUMBER INVITED	NUMBER COMING
24.			
25.			
26.			
27.			
28.			
29.			
30.			
31.			
32.			
33.			
34.			
35.			
36.			

NAME & ADDRESS	PHONE	NUMBER INVITED	NUMBER COMING
37.			
38.			
39.			
40.			
41.			
42.			
43.			
44.			
45.			
46.			
47.			
48.			

SHEVA BERACHOT CELEBRATION GUEST LIST

Date _____   Time _____

Host(s) _____   Phone/Fax _____

Address _____   Car/Cellular phone/Pager _____

City _____ State _____ Zip _____   E-mail address _____

Asterisk the name of male guest who will be giving *d'var Torah*.

NAME & ADDRESS	PHONE	NUMBER INVITED	NUMBER COMING
1.			
2.			
3.			
4.			
5.			
6.			
7.			
8.			
9.			
10.			

NAME & ADDRESS	PHONE	NUMBER INVITED	NUMBER COMING
11.			
12.			
13.			
14.			
15.			
16.			
17.			
18.			
19.			
20.			
21.			
22.			
23.			

NAME & ADDRESS	PHONE	NUMBER INVITED	NUMBER COMING
24.			
25.			
26.			
27.			
28.			
29.			
30.			
31.			
32.			
33.			
34.			
35.			
36.			

NOTES

Part V

Keeping Track of Gifts

GIFT RECORD CARDS

Ibelieve it is much easier to keep track of gifts on index cards rather than in a notebook. If you can find a prepackaged set, buy it! You will save yourself a lot of time. If you plan to type up the blank cards or have them printed, begin right now. Complete one card for each invitation sent out: one per family, unless you are friendly enough with some of the children to keep a separate card for each. File the cards alphabetically or by family, whichever is easiest for you. Remember to keep track of responses, gifts, and thank-you notes.

Name _____ R.S.V.P. _____

Address _____

City _____ State _____ Zip _____ Phone _____

Invitation: Ceremony ☐ Cocktails ☐ Reception

Gift   *Acknowledged*

Engagement _____

Shower 1 _____

Shower 2 _____

Wedding _____

REGISTERING GIFTS

Try to visit several stores with your fiancé and register gifts of special interest to one or both of you. You do not have to register at the large department stores--many outlets carry a wide variety of quality gifts and housewares at *discounted prices*. The savings (usually 25 to 70%) are well worth the time spent finding these stores! Register everything from fine china and linens to *tzatskes* (gadgets, frivolities) and crystal figurines; and don't forget Judaica items and books.

Alter the list on the following page to your personal needs and dreams. Below, fill in the names, addresses, and phone numbers of the stores where you have registered. Write the number of the store next to the gifts you would most like to receive. Remember to give the manufacturer(s) and pattern numbers of your choices of china, crystal, and so on to your mother and maid or matron of honor; they will pass along the information to any guests who ask.

Store 1 _____   Phone _____
Address _____   Fax _____
City _____   E-mail address _____
State _____ Zip _____   Internet _____
                                     Hours _____

Store 2 _____   Phone _____
Address _____   Fax _____
City _____   E-mail address _____
State _____ Zip _____   Internet _____
                                     Hours _____

Store 3 _____   Phone _____
Address _____   Fax _____
City _____   E-mail address _____
State _____ Zip _____   Internet _____
                                     Hours _____

Store 4 _____   Phone _____
Address _____   Fax _____
City _____   E-mail address _____
State _____ Zip _____   Internet _____
                                     Hours _____

Store 5 _____   Phone _____
Address _____   Fax _____
City _____   E-mail address _____
State _____ Zip _____   Internet _____
                                     Hours _____

BRIDE AND GROOM'S WISH LIST

(See also "We Already Have" List)

Kitchen, Dining Room:
Bakeware
Bread baskets
Cake-decorating set
Canister set
Cheese board
China
Chip and dip platter
Cookbooks
Crystal bowls and platters
Crystal stemware
Cutlery set(s)
Dish towels
Flatware (everyday, fancy)
Glassware
Gravy boats
Hand towels
Microwave cookware
Oven-to-table cookware
Oven mitts, potholders
Pitchers
Place mats (plastic, linen)
Punch bowl set
Salad bowl set
Salt and pepper shakers
Serving bowls
Serving platters
Serving utensils
Silver coffee/tea set
Spice rack
Table linens
Tea kettle
Towel and foil dispenser

Bathroom, Bedroom:
Bath and hand towels
Bathroom accessories
Bathroom rug ensemble
Beach towels
Bedspread, comforter
Blankets, quilts
Folding bed tray
Scale
Sheets and pillowcases
Throw rugs

Judaica:
Art objects
Bible (Hebrew or English)
Books
Candlesticks--Shabbat
Challah cover
Challah tray and knife
Elijah's cup
Etrog holder
Haggadah(s)
Havdalah set
Kiddush cups
Lulav case
Matzah cover
Matzah tray
Menorah
Mezzuzot
Seder plate
Sukkah (canvas)

Barware:
Bar tools
Cocktail shaker
Decanter
Ice bucket
Wine cooler

Miscellaneous:
Barbecue grill and cover
Barbecue utensils
Candlesticks--decorative
Crystal figurines
Decorative mirror
Exercise equipment
Lamps
Luggage
Magazine rack
Outdoor lounge chairs
Outdoor table/chairs set
Picture frames
Pictures, prints
Sports equipment
Vases
Videotape rack
Wedding memories album

Home Electronics:
Camera
Cellular phone
Clock radio
Compact disc (CD) player
Computer equipment
Computer software
Stereo equipment
Television
Telephones
Videocamera and case
Videocassette recorder (VCR)

Appliances:
Blender
Bread machine
Can opener (electric)
Clothes dryer
Coffee bean grinder
Coffee maker
Electric bread slicer
Espresso maker
Food processor
Hot tray
Microwave oven
Mixer
Mini vacuum cleaner
Popcorn popper
Refrigerator
Sewing machine
Slow cooker (crock pot)
Toaster oven
Vacuum cleaner
Waffle maker
Washing machine
Wok

"WE ALREADY HAVE" LIST

No one wants six teapots or four salad bowl sets! Use this page to write down the items that the two of you already have. You may save yourself a lot of unnecessary time returning and exchanging gifts if you help your guests out: many people *will* ask where you have registered and what you want. Give this list, in addition to the "Bride and Groom's Wish List," to your mother and maid or matron of honor. You can be much more genuine in your thanks when you really *do* love a gift!

GIFT IDEAS FOR ATTENDANTS, PARENTS, AND EACH OTHER

Attendants:

Book
Business card case
Candlesticks
Clothing accessory
Gift certificate
Jewelry
Jewish National Fund tree certificate
Judaica item
Key ring
Letter opener
Mezzuzah
Money clip
Paper weight
Pen/pencil set
Perfume or cologne
Picture frame
Stationery
Subscription to magazine
Toiletries basket

Each Other:

Jewelry
Jewelry box
Romantic evening for two
Sentimental clothing
Silver picture frame
*Tallit**
Tickets to a favorite show
Watch

Parents:

Balloon bouquet
Book
Dinner at a special place
Fancy picture frame
Flowering plant
Fruit, cheese, and/or wine basket
Judaica item
Laminated, framed invitation
Mail-order kosher food
Perfume or cologne

Child Attendants:

Book**
Bouquet of balloons
Bridal dress-up set
Candy in a decorative jar
Cassette**
Compact Disc (CD)
Framed photo from wedding
Gift certificate
Jewelry
Picture frame (lucite)
Personalized clothing
Stuffed animal
Videocassette

---

*   *Note*: A *tallit* is a traditional engagement gift from the bride to the groom.

** *K'tonton in Israel Read Along Book & Cassette* series is a good choice.

NOTES

Part VI

Wedding Day Details

HONORARY DUTIES

TENAI'IM WITNESSES

1. _____   2. _____

KETUBBAH WITNESSES

1. _____   2. _____

CHUPPAH POLE HOLDERS

1. _____   3. _____

2. _____   4. _____

SHEVA BERACHOT

Ceremony

1. _____
2. _____
3. _____
4. _____
5. _____
6. _____
7. _____

Alternate: _____

Benchen

1. _____
2. _____
3. _____
4. _____
5. _____
6. _____
7. _____

Alternate: _____

YICHUD WITNESSES

1. _____   2. _____

Music Selections

Your wedding day is very emotional and a time when your musical selections can make or break the mood. Your band leader will be your best source for guidance. He or she will help you select processional, ceremonial, and recessional music, as well as special songs for the reception, to make them both beautiful and meaningful for you. Other sources for songs are the *Mazel Tov! Music For A Jewish Wedding* book of sheet music and accompanying instrumental tape, and the *Music to Wed By* pamphlet (see p. 181). Below are listed some of the most popular Jewish songs for the processional and recessional. Remember to include songs from your childhood and songs your parents and grandparents used to sing to you when you were young, if appropriate.

Processional

It is a good idea to pick a special song for the groom, another song for the parents and attendants, and another for the bride. Unless you have a very experienced and cooperative band, it is best not to choose a different song for each person or couple in the processional.

Suggestions:

"Dodi Li"	"I Am My Beloved's"
"Iti Mi'Levanon"	"Come with Me from Lebanon"
"Hana'ava Babanot"	"Fairest Among Maidens"
"Erev Shel Shoshanim"	"Evening of Roses"
"Chorshat Haekalyptus"	"The Eucalyptus Grove"

Recessional

Make sure the instrumentalists continue to play until the last person in the recessional has walked out through the doors, so that no one will be stranded in the aisle without music!

Suggestions:

"Od Yishama"	"Again Will Be Heard"
"Simmen Tov U'mazel Tov"	"Good Fortune and Good Luck"
"Yasis Alayichn"	"May God Rejoice over You"

Be aware that "The Wedding March" from "Lohengrin" ("Here Comes the Bride") was written by Richard Wagner, an anti-Semite, for a mystical Christian wedding that was never consummated; and "Midsummer Night's Dream" (the traditional American recessional piece) was written by Felix Mendelssohn, a Jew who converted to Christianity, in celebration of a pagan wedding.

Fill your selections in here:

1. *Hachnasat Kallah*, Attending the Bride

   _____

   _____

2. Groom Walking to *Badeken die Kallah*,
   Veiling of the Bride

   _____

   _____

3. Processional

   _____

   _____

   _____

   _____

   _____

4. Ceremony

   _____

   _____

5. Recessional

   _____

   _____

   _____

   _____

   _____

   _____

   _____

6. Cocktail Reception

   _____

   _____

   _____

   _____

   _____

   _____

   _____

   _____

   _____

7. Entrance as Mr. and Mrs.

   _____

8. Reception

   Circle Dancing

   _____

   _____

   _____

   First Dance

   _____

   Other Special Songs

   _____

   _____

   _____

   _____

   _____

   _____

ITEMS THAT GO TO THE CEREMONY AND RECEPTION SITES

(Wedding Day)

BRIDE

- ☐ Bra and pantyhose
- ☐ Crinoline
- ☐ Garter
- ☐ Honeymoon suitcase
- ☐ Jewelry
- ☐ Overnight bag
- ☐ Sheet (to protect dress in the car)
- ☐ Shoes
- ☐ Veil or hat
- ☐ Wedding day toiletries bag
- ☐ Wedding dress

GROOM

- ☐ Honeymoon suitcase
- ☐ Honeymoon tickets
- ☐ *Ketubbah*
- ☐ *Kippah*
- ☐ *Kittel*
- ☐ Marriage license
- ☐ Overnight bag
- ☐ Ring(s)

Note: If you are including the *Tena'im* ceremony, be sure the rabbi has the *tena'im* paper.

PARENTS AND ATTENDANTS

To Kabbalat Panim:

- ☐ China plate to break
- ☐ Liquor, light food

To Ceremony Site:

- ☐ Bag with glass
- ☐ *Ketubbah*
- ☐ Wine cup(s)
- ☐ Wine bottle

To the Front Table (lobby):

- ☐ Fancy feather or colored pens
- ☐ Guest registry book
- ☐ *Kippot (yarmulkes)*
- ☐ Programs
- ☐ "Welcome" sign

To the Caterer:

- ☐ *Benchers*
- ☐ Cake knife
- ☐ Cocktail napkins
- ☐ Place cards

To the Head Table:

- ☐ Money bag for gift checks
- ☐ Stand for *ketubbah*

To the Ladies' Room:

- ☐ Basket of amenities

To the Men's Room:

- ☐ Basket of amenities

To Ring Bearer(s):

- ☐ Ring pillow(s)

DON'T FORGET TO BRING HOME

- ☐ Bag with glass
- ☐ Basket(s) of amenities
- ☐ *Benchers*--extras
- ☐ Bride's bouquet
- ☐ Cake knife
- ☐ Cake ornament(s)
- ☐ Cake--top layer
- ☐ Cocktail napkins--extras
- ☐ Floral centerpieces
- ☐ Gifts, cards, money bag
- ☐ Guest registry, pens
- ☐ *Ketubbah*
- ☐ *Kippot (yarmulkes)*--extras
- ☐ *Kittel*
- ☐ Leftovers from caterer
- ☐ Marriage license
- ☐ Mothers' pieces of china
- ☐ Programs--extras
- ☐ Ring pillow(s)
- ☐ *Tena'im* paper
- ☐ "Welcome" sign
- ☐ Wine bottle
- ☐ Wine cup(s)

WEDDING DAY TOILETRIES BAG

(Bride and groom should *each* have one.)

- ☐ Adhesive bandages
- ☐ Aerosol spray for wrinkles in clothes
- ☐ After-shave lotion
- ☐ Aspirin
- ☐ Baby powder
- ☐ Bobby pins (white for veil, colored for *kippot*)
- ☐ Breath spray
- ☐ Brush
- ☐ Coins for phone calls
- ☐ Comb
- ☐ Contact lens solutions
- ☐ Corsage pins
- ☐ Cosmetics
- ☐ Cotton balls
- ☐ Cotton swabs
- ☐ Curling iron
- ☐ Deodorant
- ☐ Facial tissues
- ☐ Feminine protection
- ☐ Hair dryer
- ☐ Hair spray
- ☐ Lipstick, lip gloss
- ☐ Lotion
- ☐ Manicure scissors
- ☐ Mirror
- ☐ Mousse for hair
- ☐ Nail file, clipper
- ☐ Nail polish (clear, colored)
- ☐ Needle and thread
- ☐ Pantyhose (colored, nude)
- ☐ Perfume
- ☐ Razor
- ☐ Safety pins
- ☐ Shaving cream
- ☐ Straight pins
- ☐ Toothbrush, toothpaste, cup
- ☐ White chalk to remove lipstick stains

PHOTOGRAPHIC SCHEDULE

Use these pages to organize the photographic schedule for the wedding day. It is a good idea to have many of the formal pictures taken before the ceremony, whether or not the bride and groom are seeing each other. The bride's formals take a long time and should be scheduled first. After the bride's pictures have been taken (alone, with her attendants, with her siblings, with her parents, with her grandparents, with her mother, and with her whole family), repeat the process with the groom and his family. If including young children, arrange for these photos to be taken at the end of the session. (Do your best and hope for some fun candids.) Remember to have the photographer check the coloring of the carpeting and walls in the room(s) where the pictures will be taken. It is up to him or her to provide the proper backdrop and a white sheet on the floor if the existing floor covering clashes with your wedding colors.

By spending a few minutes now to complete these pages, you will be (almost!) ensured that the right people will be present at the correct time and place to be included in their portion of the formal photographs. Make sure you have given a copy of this schedule to everyone involved, especially the photographer.

This is also a good time to look at some of your photographer's proof albums to decide which poses you do and do not want to include. (Some really *are* corny!) Your time for picture taking is relatively limited because you will be anxious to begin the ceremony or to enter the reception as "husband and wife." Review the schedule of events with the photographers and videographers to be certain that they do not miss any important parts. Refer to Part I to refresh your memory of the details.

BEFORE *KABBALAT PANIM*

Location _____ Time _____

People _____

_____

_____

_____

Location _____ Time _____

People _____

_____

_____

_____

KABBALAT PANIM

Location _____ Time _____

Events _____

_____

_____

BADEKEN

Location _____ Time _____

People _____

_____

_____

PROCESSIONAL

Location _____ Time _____

People _____

_____

_____

_____

_____

CEREMONY

(Check with your rabbi as to regulations.)

Location _____ Time _____

Events _____

_____

_____

_____

_____

RECESSIONAL

Time _____

People _____

_____

_____

_____

_____

COCKTAIL HOUR
(after *Yichud)*

Location _____ Time _____

People _____

_____

_____

_____

_____

RECEPTION

Location _____ Time _____

People _____

_____

_____

_____

_____

_____

_____

_____

_____

_____

_____

Events _____

_____

_____

_____

_____

Tables _____

_____

_____

_____

LEAVING THE RECEPTION

Location _____ Time _____

People _____

_____

_____

_____

Events _____

_____

_____

NOTES

NOTES

Part VII

Helpful Information

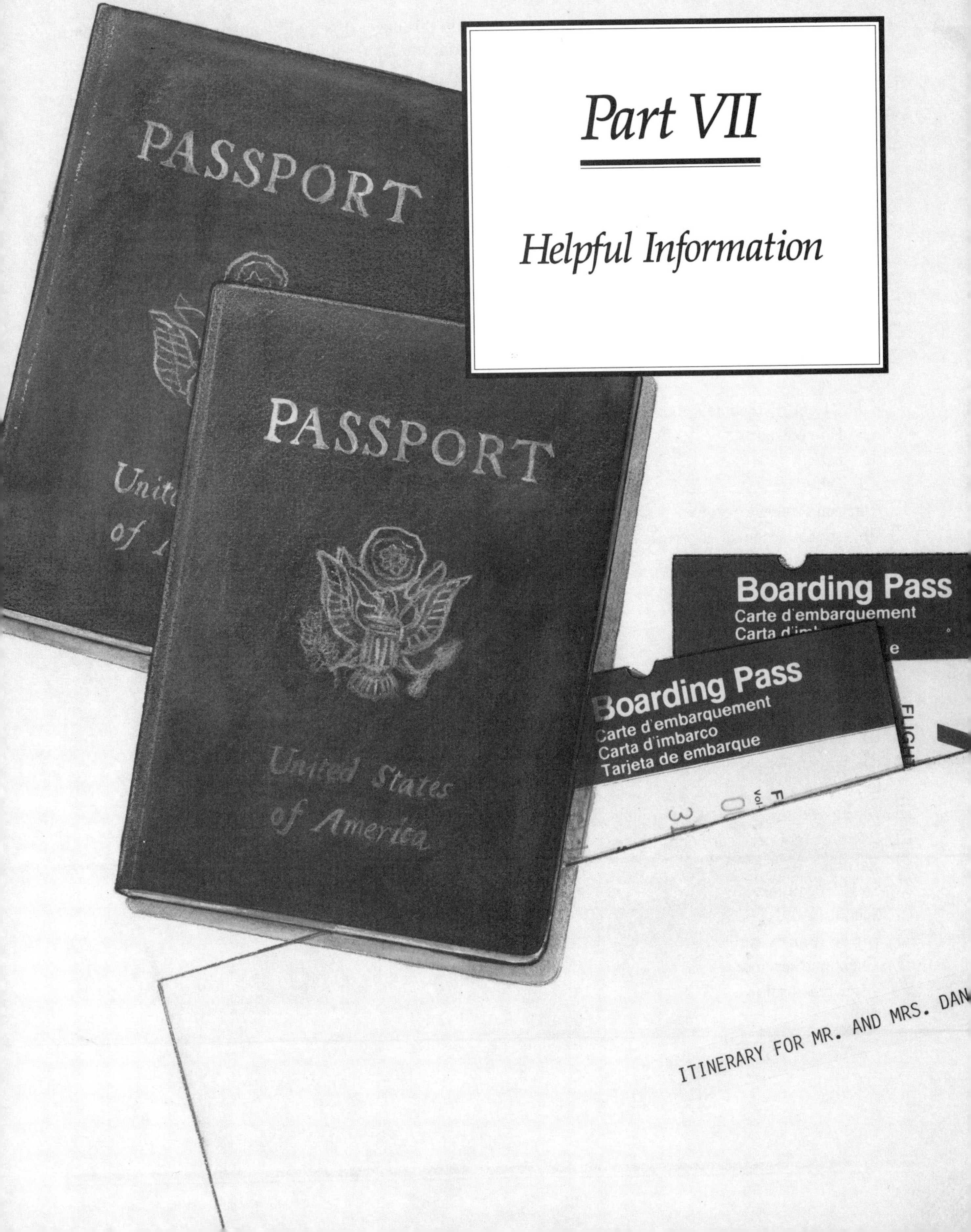

CHANGING YOUR NAME OFFICIALLY

If you have decided to retain your maiden name, you may skip this page! (If so, did you enclose an announcement to that effect with your invitation, or will you be sending one out now?)

If you are taking your groom's last name or are hyphenating your and your groom's last names, you need to make this change official on many legal documents. (Don't forget to mail your change-of-address forms.)

- ☐ Accounting department at place of employment
- ☐ Bank accounts
- ☐ Business cards and stationery
- ☐ Business licenses
- ☐ Car registration
- ☐ Computer on-line services
- ☐ Credit cards
- ☐ Driver's license
- ☐ Insurance
  - ☐ Car
  - ☐ Disability Income Protection--Hospital, Physicians, Major Medical
  - ☐ Homeowner's
  - ☐ Life
  - ☐ Other _____
- ☐ Internal Revenue Service
- ☐ Investment accounts or certificates
- ☐ Loans
- ☐ Magazine subscriptions
- ☐ Memberships
  - ☐ Associations
  - ☐ Athletic
  - ☐ Business
  - ☐ Community
  - ☐ Religious
  - ☐ University alumni organizations
  - ☐ Other _____
- ☐ Mortgage
- ☐ Passport (not necessary until needed)
- ☐ Resumé
- ☐ Safe deposit box
- ☐ School records
- ☐ Social Security card
- ☐ Telephone services
- ☐ Voter registration
- ☐ Will

OTHER THINGS YOU SHOULD KNOW

On the following pages, you will find the names, addresses, and phone number of some companies and organizations that will supply you with various information in which you may now be interested.

MAZEL TOV! MUSIC FOR A JEWISH WEDDING

A 64-page book containing 49 selections and an accompanying instrumental cassette of all selections, performed by the Neshoma Orchestra, one of the outstanding wedding bands in the United States. Book and cassette available for $29.95 plus $4.50 shipping or book and CD for $32.95 plus $4.50 shipping from:
> Tara Publications
> 8-I Music Fair Road
> Owings Mills, MD 21117
> or call (410) 654-0880
> Fax (800) TARA-403

MUSIC TO WED BY (Popular Jewish Titles)

Send $2.50 to:
> Women's League for Conservative Judaism
> 48 East 74th Street
> New York, NY 10021
> or call (800) 628-5083, (212) 628-1600

DONATING YOUR GOWN

A beautiful *mitzvah* and another way to give *tzedakah* is to donate your gown and veil (and/or mothers' or bridesmaids' gowns) to a Jewish organization or wedding gown loan service which will lend them to brides who would not otherwise have the luxury of such finery. In this way, you are sharing your joy with the other brides who will wear your gown to their *simcha*. Before making your donation, check with the agency to make sure that there is still a need and to find out what, if any, are the restrictions for the gowns (long sleeves, high neck, etc.).

> *In the United States:*
>
> Call your local Federation or Jewish Information Service for a suggestion in your area
> or a wedding gown loan service such as Libby in Baltimore, Maryland at (410) 578-1358 or
> Mrs. Cohen in Lakewood, New Jersey at (908) 370-8994.
>
> *In Israel* (22-pound maximum per package, mark "Used Clothes"):
>
> Rabbanit Bracha Kapach
> 12 Lod Street
> Jerusalem, Israel
> Telephone: 02-249-296

MAZON

For more information about this charitable organization, whose proceeds benefit world hunger, write to:
> 12401 Wilshire Boulevard, Suite 303
> Los Angeles, CA 90025-1015
> or call (310) 442-0020
> Fax (310) 442-0030

MARCH OF DIMES

Educational information available through your local March of Dimes chapter or from:
Education and Health Promotion Department
March of Dimes Birth Defects Foundation
1275 Mamaroneck Avenue
White Plains, NY 10605
or call (888) MODIMES, (914) 428-7100

TAY-SACHS DISEASE

To locate the nearest testing center and receive the free pamphlet, "What Every Family Should Know," write to:
The National Tay-Sachs & Allied Diseases Association
23 Green Street
New York, NY 10013
or call (212) 431-0431

INTERNATIONAL DRIVER'S LICENSE

Take two (2) passport-size photos, your valid driver's license, and a $10 fee to your local American Automobile Association (AAA) office. AAA can take the photos for an additional $7 (members) or $10 (non-members).

ORIGINAL DESIGN HUPPAH

Original Design Huppah offers a series of "stock" designs from which couples can choose, but their specialty is creating an original design from one of their ideas or one of the client's. Rentals are also available. For more information write to:
Original Design Huppah
25 St. Nicholas Street
Lynbrook, NY 11563
or call (516) 593-4767

©1992 by O.D.H. "Susan & Randy's Sunset"

©1992 by O.D.H.

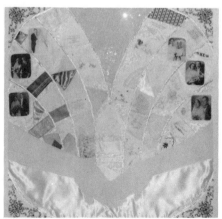

©1992 by O.D.H. "Family's Embrace"

NOTES

NOTES

DISCOUNT ORDER FORM

If you have enjoyed this *Planner*, why not order one or two to give for engagement gifts?

Please send me _____ copy(ies) of *The Complete Jewish Wedding Planner* at the reduced cost of $16.50 plus $3.50 postage and handling for a total of $20.00. (Maryland residents add $.83 sales tax.)
Make check payable to **PSP Press, Inc.**

Ship to:
Name _____ Phone _____

Address _____

City _____ State _____ Zip _____

.... (FOLD HERE SECOND, ENCLOSE CHECK, AND SEAL WITH TAPE) ....

I will be happy to contact you or a friend with more information about any topic contained with in the *Planner*.
Please call me at **(410) 486-0523**, fax any questions or comments to **(410) 486-0568** or email to **tcjwp@juno.com**.

Name _____ Phone _____

Address _____

City _____ State _____ Zip _____

Name _____ Phone _____

Address _____

City _____ State _____ Zip _____

Name _____ Phone _____

Address _____

City _____ State _____ Zip _____

.... (FOLD HERE FIRST, ENCLOSE CHECK, AND SEAL WITH TAPE) ....

Comments:

_____
_____
_____
_____
_____
_____

FROM _____

_____

_____

WENDY CHERNAK HEFTER

PSP PRESS INC

101 BRIGHTSIDE AVENUE

BALTIMORE MD 21208-4804

‖‖‖‖‖‖‖‖‖‖‖‖‖‖‖‖‖‖‖‖‖‖‖‖‖‖‖‖‖‖‖‖‖

GLOSSARY

Adar. The twelfth (and thirteenth, in leap year) month of the Hebrew
 calendar (Hebrew).
 (*Note:* The Hebrew months are counted beginning with the month of
 Nissan, the month in which Pesach falls. Biblically, the years are
 counted from Tishrei, the month in which Rosh Hashanah, the New
 Year, falls.)

Adar I, Adar II. During leap years, seven times each nineteen years,
 a second month of Adar is added to the Hebrew calendar. Adar is
 renamed Adar I and the second month is called Adar II (Hebrew).

Aliyah. Calling to the Torah (Hebrew).

Aliyot. Plural for *aliyah* (Hebrew).

"Ani le'dodi ve'dodi li." "I am my beloved's and my beloved is mine"
 (Hebrew).

Ashkenazim. Jews with Eastern European roots.

Aufruf. The groom's being called to the Torah on the Sabbath before
 his wedding, as the public announcement of his forthcoming marriage
 (German).

Av. Fifth month of the Hebrew calendar.

Badeken die Kallah. Veiling of the Bride (Yiddish).

Bar Mitzvah. Literally, son of commandment; the time in a boy's life
 (thirteen years old) when he becomes a responsible Jewish man
 (Hebrew).

Benchen. Grace After the Meal (Yiddish).

Bencher. Booklet containing the *Benchen* (Yiddish).

Beracha. Blessing (Hebrew).

Berachot. Plural for *beracha* (Hebrew).

Bet/Vet. Second letter of the Hebrew alphabet; numerological value = 2.

Bi'ah. Literally, sexual intercourse or consummation (Hebrew).

Birkat Chatanim. Blessing for grooms (Hebrew).

Birkat Erusin. Betrothal blessings (Hebrew).

Birkat Hamazon. Grace After the Meal (Hebrew).

Challah. Twisted egg bread for Sabbath, holidays, and special occasions
 (Hebrew).

Chanukah. Festival of Lights; commemoration of the rededication of the
 Temple (Hebrew).

Chasid. Member of a specific group of very observant Jews.

Chatan. Groom (Hebrew).

Chossen. Groom (Yiddish).

Chossen's Tish. Groom's Table--a preceremony custom for the groom
 (Yiddish).

Chuppah. Wedding canopy; also used synonymously with the wedding
 ceremony (Hebrew).

Cohen. Descendants of Aaron who served as the high priests in the
 Temple and acted as mediator between God and man (Hebrew).

Counting the *Omer.* Observed during the seven weeks from Passover to
 Shavuot (Hebrew).

Die Mezinke Oysgegeben. "The Youngest Has Been Given Away"; the
 song often used for the *Mezinke Tanz* (Yiddish).

D'var Torah. A short Torah lesson (Hebrew).

Ed. Witness (Hebrew).

Edim. Plural of *ed* (Hebrew).

Egoz. Nut (Hebrew).

Elijah's cup. The cup of wine set on the table during the Passover *seder* inviting Elijah the prophet as a guest (Hebrew).

Erusin. Betrothal (Hebrew).

Etrog. The citron fruit used during the holiday of *Sukkot* (Hebrew).

Glatt Kosher. Label given to food under stringent supervision (Hebrew).

Hachnassat Kallah. Attending and complimenting the bride; occurs at the same time as the *Kabbalat Panim* (Hebrew).

Haftorah. Portion from Prophets (Hebrew).

Haggadah. The book containing the story of Passover, recited at the *Pesach Seder* (Hebrew).

Hakafot. Processionals on Hoshanah Rabbah and Simchat Torah (Hebrew).

Halacha. Jewish Law (Hebrew).

Halachically. According to Jewish Law (Hebrew).

Harei At. Groom's wedding vow to bride (Hebrew).

"Harei at me'kudeshet li b'tabba'at zu ke'dat Moshe ve'Yisrael." "Behold, you are consecrated unto me with this ring in accordance with the law of Moses and Israel." (Hebrew).

"Harei ata me'kudash li." The masculine version of the Harei At (Hebrew).

Havdalah. Ceremony marking the end of the Sabbath (Hebrew).

Hoshanah Rabbah. Seventh day of Sukkot (Hebrew).

Jewish Wedding Planner. Bride, her mother or this book.

Kabbalat Panim. Literally, greeting of faces; groom's preceremony reception (Hebrew).

Kaddish. Memorial Prayer (Hebrew).

Kallah. Bride (Hebrew, Yiddish).

"Kallah na'eh va'chasudah." "A pretty and joyous bride" (Hebrew).

Kashrut. Laws of keeping kosher (Hebrew).

Kesef. Money (Hebrew).

Ketubbah. Jewish marriage contract (Hebrew).

Ketubbot. Plural of *ketubbah* (Hebrew).

Kichel. Egg cookies (Yiddish).

Kiddush. Prayer of sanctification; refreshments, reception (Hebrew).

Kiddushin. Betrothal, engagement, sanctification (Hebrew).

Kinyan. Formal acceptance of conditions, such as the groom's acceptance of the *ketubbah* (Hebrew).

Kippah. Skullcap (Hebrew).

Kippot. Plural of *kippah* (Hebrew).

Kisei Kallah. Bridal throne, *Badeken* chair (Hebrew).

"Ki tov." "It was good" (Hebrew).

Kittel. White robe worn by the groom (Hebrew).

Kosher. Suitable according to Jewish dietary laws (Hebrew).

K'tonton. Sadie Rose Weilerstein's Jewish thumb-sized storybook character (Hebrew).

Kuf. Twentieth letter of the Hebrew alphabet; numerological value = 100 (Hebrew).

Lag B'Omer. Thirty-third day of the counting of the Omer (Hebrew).

Lamed. Twelfth letter of the Hebrew alphabet; numerological value = 30 (Hebrew).

"L'chaim." "To life!" Traditional Jewish toast (Hebrew).

Lev. Heart; numerological value = 32 (Hebrew).

Levite. Descendants of the tribe of Levi who helped the Cohanim (pl.) in the Temple (Hebrew).

Lulav. Used with the *etrog* during *Sukkot*, this palm branch is made from a shoot of a palm tree, three twigs of myrtle and two willow branches (Hebrew).

Maftir. Last *aliyah* of Shabbat morning Torah reading (Hebrew).

Mashgiach. Supervisor of *kashrut* (Hebrew).

Matzah. Unleavened bread eaten on Pesach (Hebrew).

Mazal. Luck (Hebrew).

Mazel. Luck (Yiddish).

"Mazal tov." "Good luck" (Hebrew).

"Mazel tov." "Good luck" (Yiddish).

Mazon. Literally, sustenance; also, a Jewish organization whose goal is to raise awareness among Jews about world hunger and to raise money for Jews and non-Jews worldwide (Hebrew).

Menorah. The eight-branched candelabrum used on Chanukah (Hebrew).

Mezinke Tanz. Dance by the bride and groom in honor of the occasion of their parents' marrying off the last child in the family (Yiddish).

Mezzuzah. Tiny scroll of parchment with the *Shema Yisrael* written on it, inside a case; mounted on the doorposts of Jewish homes (Hebrew).

Mikvah. Ritual bath (Hebrew).

Minyan. Ten men over Bar Mitzvah age (Hebrew).

Mitzvah. Literally, commandment; good deed (Hebrew).

Mitzvah l'sameach chatan v'kallah. The good deed of making the bride and groom happy during the ceremony (Hebrew).

Motzi. Blessing over bread (Hebrew).

Nachas. Joy (Yiddish).

Ner. Candle (Hebrew).

Nissuin. Wedding ceremony (Hebrew).

"Orah ve'simchah ve'sasson ve'yikar." "Light and gladness and joy and honor" (Hebrew).

Panim chadashot. New faces (Hebrew).

Passover. The seven-day holiday celebrating the Israelites' freedom from slavery by the Egyptians.

Perutah. Smallest coin in ancient times (Hebrew).

"Pe'ru ure'vu." "Be fruitful and multiply" (Hebrew).

Pesach. Passover (Hebrew).

Rosh Chodesh. First day of a new Hebrew month (Hebrew).

Rosh Hashanah. Jewish New Year (Hebrew).

Ruskah. Specially baked bread Israelis often break over the newlyweds' heads (Hebrew).

Seder. Literally, order; the ceremonial dinner on the first and second nights of *Pesach* when the *Haggadah* is read (Hebrew).

Semachot. Plural of *simcha* (Hebrew).

Sephardim. Jews of Spanish and Portuguese descent (Hebrew).

Se'udah. Festive meal, celebration (Hebrew).

Shabbat. Sabbath (Hebrew).

Shadchan. Matchmaker (Hebrew).

Shalom Bayit. Peace in the house (Hebrew).

Shavuot. Pentecost (Hebrew).

Sheloshim. Thirty days after burial (Hebrew).

Shema Yisrael. Literally, Hear O Israel; the beginning of one of the holiest Jewish prayers, which declares faith in God (Hebrew).

Shetar. Deed (Hebrew).

Sheva. Seven (Hebrew).

Sheva Berachot. Seven Blessings; part of the wedding ceremony and the Birkat Hamazon at the wedding reception (Hebrew).

Shevat. Eleventh month of the Hebrew calendar (Hebrew).

Shlemut. Wholeness (Hebrew).

Shomer Shabbat. Sabbath observer (Hebrew).

Shoshvinim. Literally, best men; entourage (Hebrew).

Shulchan Aruch. Code of Jewish law (Hebrew).

Shushan Purim. Fifteenth day of Adar, the day after Purim (Hebrew).

Simcha. Joyous occasion (Hebrew, Yiddish).

Simchas. Plural (anglicized) for *simcha* (Yiddish).

Sitting *Shiva.* Observing the week of mourning (Hebrew).

Sivan. Third month of the Hebrew calendar (Hebrew).

Sofer. Scribe (Hebrew).

Sukkah. A temporary dwelling constructed for the seven-day holiday of *Sukkot* (Hebrew).

Sukkot. Tabernacles, Feast of Booths (Hebrew).

Tabba'at. Ring (Hebrew).

Tallit. Prayer shawl (Hebrew).

Talmud. Compilation of Jewish law and commentaries, comprised of the Mishna and the Gemara (Hebrew).

Tammuz. Fourth month of the Hebrew calendar (Tammuz).

Tay-Sachs disease. A fatal genetic disorder in children that causes the progressive destruction of the central nervous system.

Tefillin. Phylacteries (Hebrew).

Tena'im. Literally, conditions; terms of engagement arrangement (Hebrew).

Tevet. Tenth month of the Hebrew calendar (Hebrew).

Tevilah. Ceremonial immersion in a mikvah (Hebrew).

Tisha B'Av. Ninth day of Av, commemorating the destruction of the Temple (Hebrew).

Tishrei. Seventh month of the Hebrew calendar (Hebrew).

Tov. Good (Hebrew).

Tzatskes. Gadgets, frivolities (Yiddish).

Tzedakah. Charity (Hebrew).

Tzniut. Modesty and separation of males and females in public (Hebrew).

"Ve'erastich." "And I will betroth you" (Hebrew).

"Ve'kanina." "I have made a *kinyan*"; last word completed in the *ketubbah* (Hebrew).

Yarmulke. Skullcap (Yiddish).

Yichud. Seclusion (Hebrew).

Yom Ha'atzma'ut. Israel's Independence Day (Hebrew).

Yom Kippur. Day of Atonement (Hebrew).

Yomim tovim. Plural for *yom tov* (Hebrew).

Yom tov. Literally, good day; holiday (Hebrew).

Yom Yerushalayim. Jerusalem Reunification Day (Hebrew).

BIBLIOGRAPHY

Birnbaum, Philip. *A Book of Jewish Concepts.* New York: Hebrew
  Publishing, 1975.

Cardozo, Arlene Rossen. *Jewish Family Celebrations.* New York: St.
  Martin's Press, 1982.

Dellwood Books. *Personal Party Planner.* New York: Crown, 1982.

Diamant, Anita. *The New Jewish Wedding.* New York: Summit Books, 1985.

Editors of *Bride's* Magazine, with Kathy C. Mullins. *Bride's Book of
  Etiquette.* New York: Putnam, 1984.

Editors of *Bride's* Magazine. *Bride's Wedding Planner.* New York:
  Fawcett Columbine Books, 1980.

Editors of *Modern Bride*, with Stephanie Dahl. *Modern Bride Guide to
  Your Wedding and Marriage.* New York: Ziff-Davis, 1984.

Eisenstadt, Merrie M. "Grooms with a View." *Washington Jewish
  Week, Wonderful Weddings* section. Rockville, MD. February 20, 1992,
  pp. 4, 12.

Encyclopedia Judaica. Jerusalem: Keter, 1971, pp. 1026-1054.

Five Megilloth. New York: Soncino Press, 1971.

Freudenheim, Ellen. *The Executive Bride.* New York: Cloverdale Press, 1985.

Fried, Stephen. "Ask These 10 Questions." *Baltimore Jewish Times
  Style Magazine.* vol. 203, no. 2, January 7, 1992. pp 76-79.

Friedman, Sally. "Heart and Home." *Baltimore Jewish Times Style
  Magazine.* vol. 203, no. 2, January 7, 1992. pp. 22-26.

Ganzfried, Rabbi Solomon. *Code of Jewish Law--Kitzur Shulchan Aruch.*
  New York: Hebrew Publishing, 1981.

Gold, Sharon. "Wedding Notebook." Women's Day 101 Wedding Ideas
  for Brides, 1986, vol. 13, pp. 65-80.

Goldin, Hyman E. *The Jewish Woman and Her Home.* New York:
  Hebrew Publishing, 1941.

Goss, Dinah Braun, and Schwartz, Marla Schram. *The Bride's Guide.*
  New York: Red Dembner Enterprises, 1983.

Hager, Rachel (editor). "Welcome to the Atrium - The Jewish
  Wedding." *Atrium of Spring Valley.* August, 1995.

Hofman, Ethel. "Today's Trends." *Baltimore Jewish Times*, vol. 230,
  no. 3, July 19, 1996. pp. 30-32.

The Holy Scriptures. Philadelphia: Jewish Publication Society of America,
  1955.

Israel, Richard J. "Rites (and Wrongs) of Spring." *Moment*. June 1985, pp. 54-55.

The Jewish Encyclopedia. New York and London: Funk and Wagnalls Co., 1903, vol. V, p.261; vol. VIII, p. 205.

Kaplan, Aryeh. *Made in Heaven: A Jewish Wedding Guide*. New York: Moznaim, 1983.

Kolatch, Alfred J. *The Jewish Book of Why*. New York: Jonathan David Publishers, 1981.

Lamb, Jennifer. "Something Borrowed." *Baltimore Jewish Times Style Magazine*. vol. 203, no. 2, January 7, 1992. pp. 86-87.

Lamm, Maurice. *The Jewish Way in Love and Marriage*. New York: Harper & Row, 1980.

Latner, Helen. *Your Jewish Wedding*. New York: Doubleday, 1985.

Lempert, Barbara. "Why? The Origin of Jewish Wedding Customs." *Jewish Times/Jewish Exponent*, Wedding Section. Philadelphia, PA. 13/14, June 1985, p. W10.

Magida, Arthur J. "A Tax on Bar Mitzvahs?" *Baltimore Jewish Times*, December 27, 1985, p. 30.

The Pentateuch & Haftorahs. London: Soncino Press, 1978.

The Psalms. London: Soncino Press, 1971.

Rockland, Mae Shafter. *The Jewish Party Book*. New York: Schocken Books, 1978.

Roth, Cecil, and Wigoder, Geoffrey. *The New Standard Jewish Encyclopedia*. Garden City, New York: Doubleday & Company, Inc., 1970.

Routtenberg, Lilly S., and Seldin, Ruth R. *The Jewish Wedding Book*. New York: Harper & Row, 1967.

Siegel, Richard, Strassfeld, Michael, and Strassfeld, Sharon. *The Jewish Catalog*. Philadelphia: Jewish Publication Society of America, 1973.

"Style 1992 Brides." *Baltimore Jewish Times*. Baltimore, MD. vol. 203, no. 22, January 7, 1992.

Wedding Pages. Omaha, NE: Wedding Information Network, Inc., 1990.

Woods, Marjorie Binford. *Your Wedding--How to Plan and Enjoy It*. New York: Berkley, 1985.

NOTES

NOTES